George Eliot's
Adam Bede

Adapted for the stage by
Geoffrey Beevers

Samuel French —London
New York — Sydney — Toronto — Hollywood

© 1990 BY GEOFFREY BEEVERS

1. *This play is fully protected under the Copyright Laws of the British Commonwealth of Nations, the United States of America and all countries of the Berne and Universal Copyright Conventions.*

2. *All rights, including Stage. Motion Picture, Radio, Television, Public Reading, and Translation into Foreign Languages, are strictly reserved.*

3. **No part of this publication may lawfully be reproduced in ANY form or by any means — photocopying, typescript, recording (including video-recording), manuscript, electronic, mechanical, or otherwise, or be transmitted or stored in a retrieval system, without prior permission.**

4. Rights of Performance by Amateurs are controlled by SAMUEL FRENCH LTD, 52 FITZROY STREET, LONDON W1P 6JR, and they, or their authorized agents, issue licences to amateurs on payment of a fee. It is an infringement of the Copyright to give any performance or public reading of the play before the fee has been paid and the licence issued.

5. Licences are issued subject to the understanding that it shall be made clear in all advertising matter that the audience will witness an amateur performance; that the names of the authors of the plays shall be included on all announcements and on all programmes: and that the integrity of the author's work will be preserved.

The Royalty Fee indicated below is subject to contract and subject to variation at the sole discretion of Samuel French Ltd.

Basic fee for each and every
performance by amateurs   Code L
in the British Isles

In Theatres or Halls seating Six Hundred or more the fee will be subject to negotiation.

In Territories Overseas the fee quoted above may not apply. A fee will be quoted on application to our local authorized agent, or if there is no such agent, on application to Samuel French Ltd, London.

6. The Professional Repertory Rights in this play are controlled by SAMUEL FRENCH LTD

The publication of this play does not imply that it is necessarily available for performance by amateurs or professionals, either in the British Isles or Overseas. Amateurs and professionals considering a production are strongly advised in their own interests to apply to the appropriate agents for consent before starting rehearsals or booking a theatre or hall.

ISBN 0 573 11049 2

Reproduced and printed by Halstan & Co. Ltd., Amersham, Bucks., England

ADAM BEDE

This adaptation was first performed on February 9th, 1990, at the Orange Tree Theatre, Richmond with the following cast:

Dinah Morris	Karen Ascoe
Adam Bede	Brian Hickey
Lisbeth Bede/Mrs Poyser	Caroline John
Capt. Arthur Donnithorne/Seth Bede	Timothy Watson
Hetty Sorrel	Cathryn Bradshaw
Mr Irwine/Mr Poyser/Bartle Massey	David Timson

Other parts were played by members of the company

The play was directed by Geoffrey Beevers
Designed by Celia Perkins

The action takes place begins in the summer of 1799 ←

The running time should be just under three hours, including a fifteen minute interval

CHARACTERS

Adam Bede, a carpenter
Lisbeth Bede, his mother
Seth Bede, his brother
Mr Poyser, a farmer
Mrs Poyser, his wife
Dinah Morris, a methodist lay preacher, and Mrs Poyser's niece
Hetty Sorrel, Mr Poyser's niece
Captain Arthur Donnithorne, the heir to the estate
The Reverend Mr Irwine, the parson
Bartle Massey, the schoolmaster
Bill
Mary Burge
Shepherd
Windsor Landlord
Windsor Landlady
Old Woman
Sarah Stone
John Olding
Counsel
Judge
Hangman
Various landlords, coachmen, servants, villagers etc.

[handwritten: Order of Appearance]

In the first production the parts were divided as follows:

Actor 1/Dinah/Mary Burge/Old Woman (page 43)**/Lady** (page 44)**/Woman** (page 47)**/Counsel**

Actor 2/Adam/Cartdriver/Shepherd/Servant (page 53)

Actor 3/Lisbeth/Mrs Poyser/Stratford Lady/Windsor Landlady/A Woman (page 44)**/3rd Woman** (page 47)**/Sarah Stone/Woman** (page 57)

Actor 4/Seth/Arthur/Bill/Landlord/WindsorCoachman/Man (page 47)**/John Olding/Hangman**

Actor 5/Hetty/Girl/2nd Woman (page 47)**/Driver** (page 53)

Actor 6/Mr Irwine/Mr Poyser/Bartle Massey/Coachman/Clerk/Windsor Landlord/Judge/Man (page 57)

INTRODUCTION

This play was commissioned by the Orange Tree Theatre in Richmond, for six actors. I was first drawn to it by the challenge of handling a huge theme in an intimate space, which I'd always enjoyed so much there as an actor. I've tried to bring the dramatic heart of the book to the theatre as faithfully as I can in one evening: to capture at least the momentum of its powerful story, and the essence of what I believe George Eliot meant by it.

Six actors provide the smallest possible cast, when the ten main parts are divided as in the original production. It could of course be done as successfully with ten actors in those parts, or with an even larger cast if desired; there are over thirty speaking parts. But there is considerable fun to be had from some doubling. For example at the birthday feast, Arthur may slip off his military coat to become Seth, then turn in his tracks to become Bill; the actress playing Dinah may become Mary Burge by the addition of a summery hat; Mr Irwine may throw off a coat to become Mr Poyser, pick up a stick to become Bartle Massey, and then become Mr Poyser again all in quick succession, so that the Chase seems full of people. This can be a delight for an audience. There are also many ironies to be gained from doubling in minor roles. Perhaps the driver who brings Arthur home to his estates may remind us of Hetty; the servant who brings Mr Irwine's fateful letter to him may seem like Adam; Hetty's hangman could almost be Arthur. On the other hand, a larger cast, if available, might well help to add to the feeling of a broader community, at funerals, marriages, dances and executions. What is most important is that the telling of the story is never held up by any costume changes or lengthy entrances.

The theatre for which I wrote the play is a small theatre in the round, where the actors could sit in the entrance corners almost among the audience when not required for the action. The actors were therefore at hand to make an entrance from the right place, or to change the scene, or simply stand forward a little to give George Eliot's comments on the action. In a proscenium theatre the same can be achieved by having the actors permanently on stage, seated at the edge of a defined acting area. This presence will not be distracting provided that they listen to the play. The act of standing and coming into the centre becomes an entrance.

Each different location, must of course, be fully and clearly imagined by the actors. The physical setting can then be achieved by as little as a table, two benches, a chair and two stools. A kitchen table can then be not only a table, but a coach, a desk, a cart, or a scaffold. A bench can become a coffin ← or a bed, a sofa or an ottoman. An actor moving a single chair from one place on the stage to another can create the difference between the Bedes' cottage and Hall Farm. Let the imagination of the actors then create a fireplace, a mirror, some plates on a shelf, or a glimpse through a doorway.

More furniture or design may of course be employed, provided they never hold up the action.

In the same spirit, as many props as are needed may be used. Perhaps tipping a driver may not necessarily require searching for a real coin, but sharing the bread and wine may be felt to be significant enough to require a real cup and some bread. Telling the story clearly should always be paramount.

The story is told within the scenes themselves. But there is another voice increasingly present: the distinctive voice of George Eliot. It should on no account be considered as a separate character but should be shared among the members of the cast, the actors taking a paragraph each and talking directly to the audience. I've shown in the text how it was first divided. The general rule should be that the actor playing the character in question, or otherwise most suitable, should take the comment. It should work to give ironic, witty or humorous insights into the action; perhaps, sometimes, like a Greek chorus, to give a wider sense of the community; and then, as the play goes on, to give those deeper insights into love and suffering which are George Eliot's special vision. These are not "Victorian moralising", but sharp, fresh insights into the immediate action we are watching.

The aim in the theatre should be to bring the imagination of the writer, as vividly as our imaginations can grasp it, to the imagination of a live audience. In the case of a writer as great as George Eliot that is surely worth trying.

My thanks especially to Sam Walters, for all his help and encouragement, and to the exceptionally talented cast who gave the play its first life.

Geoffrey Beevers

ACT I

The cast come in some five minutes before the play is due to start. They may discreetly take their places around the acting area, but without bringing the audience to silence

When the play is due to begin: Dinah Morris, a Methodist lay preacher comes forward and talks to everyone (actors and audience alike)

Dinah (*very simply*) Jesus Christ said he came to preach the Gospel to the poor. I don't know whether you ever thought about those words much? (*Slight pause*) Why, you and me, dear friends, are poor. We've been brought up in poor cottages, and have been reared on oat-cake and lived coarse; and we haven't been to school much, nor read books. Can God take much notice of us poor people? Perhaps he only made the world for the great and the wise and the rich?

A murmur from the audience. The House Lights fade

But you see Jesus spent his time almost all in doing good to poor people. He made friends of poor workmen and taught them, and took pains with them. Not but what he did good to the rich too, for he was full of love to all men, only he saw as the poor were more in want of his help. So he cured the sick and the blind and he worked miracles to feed the hungry, and he spoke very tenderly to poor sinners that were sorry for their sins.

One man in particular is listening: Seth Bede

He said "I came to save that which was lost" and he said "I came not to call the righteous, but sinners to repentance." The lost! . . . Sinners! . . . Ah, dear friends, does that mean you and me?

SCENE 1

The Bedes' cottage

Lisbeth sits

Adam enters

Adam Where's Father?

1

Lisbeth Well, Adam my lad, it's gone seven by th' clock. Thee't allays stay at Burges workin' . . . (*She rises*) Thee wants thy supper, I'll warrant. Where's thy brother? Gone arter some o's chapellin' I reckon?

Adam Ay, Seth's at no harm, Mother, thee mayst be sure. He went to the Green to hear Dinah Morris preach. But where's Father? . . . (*Pause*) Hasn't he done the coffin he promised?

Lisbeth Done the coffin?

Adam There's the stuff standing just as I left it this morning.

Lisbeth Eh, my lad, he went off to Treddleston this forenoon, an's niver come back. I doubt he's got to th' *Waggin Overthrow* again.

Adam throws off his jacket

What art goin' to do, Adam? Thee wouldstna go to work again wi' out ha'in' thy bit o' supper?

Adam is angry as he takes the wood out to his workshop

Nay, my lad, there's the taters just as thee lik'st 'em. I saved 'em o' purpose for thee. Come an'——

Adam Let be!

Lisbeth ——ha' thy supper, come.

Adam returns

Adam It's fine talking about having supper when here's a coffin promised to be ready at Broxton by seven o' clock tomorrow morning and not a nail struck yet. My throat's too full to swallow victuals.

Lisbeth Why thee canstna' get the coffin ready. It ud' take thee all night.

Adam What signifies how long it takes me? Isn't the coffin promised? Can they bury a man without a coffin?——

Lisbeth Thee't work thyself to a——

Adam I'd work my right hand off sooner than deceive with lies i' that way——

Lisbeth But thee——

Adam It makes me mad to think on't! I shall overrun these doings before long, I've stood enough of 'em.

There is a pause

Lisbeth Nay my lad, my lad, thee wouldstna go away an' break thy mother's heart an' leave thy feyther to ruin. He war a good feyther to thee. He taught thee thy trade o' carpenterin', an's niver gen me a blow, nor so much as an ill word—no not even in's drink. Thee wouldstna ha'm go th'workhus—thy own feyther.

Adam Now Mother, don't cry and talk so. I hate to be talking where it's no use.

Lisbeth But thee't allays so hard upo' thy feyther, Adam.

Adam If I wasn't sharp with him, he'd sell every bit o' stuff in the yard and spend it on drink. Now leave me alone, Mother, and let me get on with the work.

He goes out

Lisbeth hesitates to say more and sits again. There is a pause

Lisbeth (*calling*) Thy supper stans ready for thee when thee lik'st.

The only reply is the sound of Adam hammering

SCENE 2

The Green

Dinah is at the end of her talk to the villagers

Dinah Think what great blessedness it is — to know that nothing — no, not if the earth was to be burnt up, or the waters come and drown us — nothing could part us from God who loves us and who fills our souls with peace and joy. Dear friends, come and take this blessedness. It is not like the riches of this world, so that the more one gets, the less the rest can have. God is without end, his love is without end. (*Singing*)

> "Its streams the whole creation reach" — sing with me —
> "So plenteous is the store
> Enough for all, enough for each
> Enough for evermore."

Thank you, dear friends.

The meeting breaks up and the villagers disperse

Seth alone approaches her

Seth Dinah . . .

Dinah turns

You've quite made up your mind to go back to Snowfield o' Saturday, Dinah?

Dinah Yes, I'm called there, Seth. I opened the Bible for direction. If it wasn't for that clear showing of the Lord's will, I should be loath to go, for my heart yearns after my aunt and uncle and their little ones, and that poor wandering lamb, Hetty Sorrel.

Seth I think Adam's heart is set on her, and yet I cannot think as Hetty'd make him happy. It's a deep mystery the way the heart of man turns to one woman out of all the rest he's seen in the world . . . (*Slight pause*) May happen you'll think me over-bold, to speak to you about it again, but ——

Dinah Seth Bede, I thank you for your love towards me, but my heart is not free to marry. I've not turned a deaf ear to your words, Seth, for when I saw as your love was given to me, I thought it might be a leading of Providence for me to change my way of life. But God draws my heart another way. I seem to have no room for wants of my own, it's pleased God to fill my heart so with the sufferings of his poor people.

The light is fading

Seth Well, Dinah, I must seek for strength to bear it. But I feel now how weak my faith is. It seems as if, when you are gone, I could never joy in anything any more. I think it's something passing the love of women as I feel for you, for I could be content without your marrying me, if I could go and live at Snowfield and be near you.

Dinah No, Seth. Don't lightly leave your own country and kindred. It's a bleak and barren country there, not like this. We must be guided. You'll be continually in my prayers.

She presses his hand and exits

Seth (*looking after her*) Farewell!

The Actors now talk directly to the audience

G. Eliot/Actor 3 Seth and Dinah were Methodists of a very old fashioned kind

G. Eliot/Actor 1 Still, it's possible, thank Heaven, to have very erroneous theories, and very sublime feelings.

G. Eliot/Actor 4 So Seth is resolving, as he walks homeward under the solemn starlight, to repress his sadness, to be less bent on having his own will, and live more for others as Dinah does.

SCENE 3

The Bedes' cottage

The sound of hammering, Lisbeth sits in her chair. The Lights are quite dim. The hammering stops

Adam enters

Adam Donna thee sit up, Mother. I'll see to Father when he comes home.
Lisbeth Nay, I'll bide ——
Adam Maybe he wonna come at all tonight. He'll sleep off his drunkenness at the *Waggin Overthrow* again. I shall be easier if thee't in bed.
Lisbeth Nay, I'll bide till Seth comes.

There is a moment

Adam exits and resumes hammering

Lisbeth dozes until suddenly:

Seth enters

Seth The brook's fine and full now.
Lisbeth (*rising*) Seth.
Seth Another day's rain and we should have to go round by the road. Why, Mother, how is it as Father's working so late?
Lisbeth It's none of thy father — thee might know if thy head warna full o'

chapellin'. It's thy brother as does iverything, for there's niver nobody
else . . .

Seth goes over to the workshop doorway

Seth Addy, how's this? Father's forgot the coffin?
Adam Ay, lad, th' old tale; but I shall get it done.

Adam comes out to see Seth

Why, what's the matter with thee? Thee't in trouble?   it's
Seth Yes, Addy, but what must be borne and can't be helped.   ∧   ←

Adam is about to speak, but decides against it

Let me take my turn now and do thee go to bed.
Adam No lad, I'd rather go on now I'm in harness. Thee't help me to carry
it to Broxton when it's done. I'll call thee up at sunrise. Go and eat thy
supper and shut the door, so as I mayn't hear Mother's talk.

Adam exits

Lisbeth brings a lamp and some food for Seth. They sit. Adam is heard sawing

Lisbeth He's been so sore and angered he wouldn't ate — an' he's been a'
threatenin' to go away again an' I'm fast sure he'll go some dawning afore
I'm up and niver let me know. An' I'd better niver ha' had a son, and me
to be parted from him and niver see 'im no more.
Seth Come, Mother, donna grieve thyself in vain. He may say such a thing
when he's in wrath, but think how he's stood by us all, turning his earnin's
into wood for Father, when many a young man like him 'ud ha been
married and settled before now.
Lisbeth Donna talk to me about's marryin'. He's set's heart on that Hetty
Sorrel, a bit of a wench as is o' no more use nor the gillyflower on the wall.
An' to think as he might ha' Mary Burge, an' be took partners wi' Master
Burge. An' he so wise at bookin' and figurin', an' not to know no better
nor that.
Seth But Mother, thee know'st we canna love just where other folks 'ud
have us. There's nobody but God can control the heart of man. We can
only pray to——
Lisbeth Thy prayin'! Th' Methodies'll niver make thee half the man thy
brother is.
Seth It's partly truth, Mother. Adam's far above me. God distributes
talents as he sees good. But thee mustna undervally prayer. If thee
would'st pray and trust in God, thee wouldstna be so uneasy about things.
Lisbeth Unaisy! I'm i' th' right on't to be unaisy. Take no thought for the
morrow — that's what thee't allays sayin', an' what comes on't? Why, as
Adam has to take thought for thee.
Seth Those are the words o' the Bible, Mother. They mean we shouldn't be
over anxious.
Lisbeth Adam doesna pick on that tex'. I can understan' the tex' as he's
allays a-sayin' "God helps them as helps theirsens."

Seth Nay Mother, that's no text o' the Bible. It comes out of a book as Adam picked up at the stall at Treddleston.

Lisbeth Well, how'm I to know? It sounds like a tex'.

Seth (*pushing his food aside*) Let me pray a bit wi' thee before bed, for all of us. It'll comfort thee happen more than thee thinkst.

Lisbeth Well, I've nothin' to say again' it.

They pray

Seth Let us pray for poor wandering Father . . . and those who are sorrowing for him at home . . . Let us pray that Adam may never be called upon to set up his tent in a far country . . . and that his mother may be cheered and comforted by his presence all the days of her pilgrimage.

Lisbeth cries

Amen. (*He gets up and goes over to the workshop doorway and calls to Adam*) Wilt only lie down for an hour or two and let me go on the while?

Adam No, Seth, no. Make Mother go to bed and go thyself.

Lisbeth and Seth clear away

Lisbeth takes a plate out to Adam

Lisbeth Thee cans't pick a bit while thee't workin'.

Adam Ay, Mother.

Lisbeth enters and then exits with Seth

There is a pause. The stage is empty and dark, apart from the lamplight

Adam comes in for something. He hears a sharp rap at the door

What's that? (*Puzzled, he walks across*) Father?

G. Eliot/Actor 1 Outside the cottage, all was still. The light of the stars showed the placid fields on both sides of the swollen brook — quite empty of visible life.

Adam goes back to his work

There is another sharp rap on the door

G. Eliot/Actor 3 Adam's mother had told him of just such a sound coming as a sign when someone was dying. The rap of a willow-wand at the door.

Adam goes slowly across to look

G. Eliot/Actor 1 But again all was still and there was nothing but the dew-laden grass in front of the cottage.

Adam returns to work

He resolved not to open the door again.

Perhaps there is the sound of heavy rain until the stage slowly lightens

G. Eliot/Actor 4 By daylight the work was done, and the promise redeemed.

Seth and Lisbeth enter

Seth goes off to help Adam carry through the completed coffin

She clears away the food and the lamp, and then settles in her chair

Lisbeth It's a good step to Broxton . . . (*Pause*) The feyther'll happen come
in arter a bit. Not as he'll ate much. He swallers sixpennorth o' ale and
saves a ha'porth o' porridge — that's his way o' layin' by money, as I've
told 'im many a time. Eh, poor mon, he takes it quiet enough, there's no
denyin' that. (*She hears a cry and rises in alarm*)

Adam enters, pale with horror

They look at each other. Lisbeth rushes towards him, starting to scream

Seth enters

Adam It's Father — He's tumbled into the brook. Seth and me are going to
carry him in. Get a blanket.

They start to move apart, then freeze

G. Eliot/Actor 1 When death has come it is never our tenderness that we
repent of, but our severity.
Adam. (*to himself*) I was too hard on him, too hard.

SCENE 4

The Hall Farm kitchen, with bright sunlight

G. Eliot/Actor 4 Across the village of Hayslope lies The Hall Farm.
G. Eliot/Actor 1 At the Hall Farm, Dinah is staying ——
G. Eliot/Actor 3 — with her Aunt Poyser's family ——
G. Eliot/Actor 5 — and her cousin Hetty Sorrel.

Mrs Poyser is busy ironing or polishing. While Dinah is mending

Mrs Poyser I'd be glad to give you a home as an aunt should, Dinah, if
you'd come and live in this country, where folks don't live on the naked
hills like poultry a' scratching; and then you might get married to some
decent man, and there'd be plenty ready to have you if you'd only leave
off that preaching. Even Seth Bede, as is a Methodist. I know your uncle
'ud help you with a pig and very like a cow.

Dinah smiles and shakes her head

But where's the use o' talking, if you wonna be persuaded. If everybody
was like you, talking as we must despise the things o' the world, as you
say, I should like to know where the pick o' the stock and the best new
milk cheeses 'ud have to go. (*She shouts off stage*) Hetty! Take care wi' that
butter! And keep your eye on that child . . .
Dinah Nay, dear aunt, you never heard me say that all people are called to
forsake their work and their families. We can all be servants of God
wherever our lot is cast, but he gives us different sorts of work. I can no
more help spending my life in trying to do what I can for the souls of

others than you could help running if you heard your little Totty crying at the other end of the house; the voice would go to your heart and you'd hurry to help her.

Mrs Poyser (*rising*) Ah! I might as well talk to the running brook, an' tell it to stan' still. (*She looks out*) If there isn't the young squire and the Rector a' coming into the yard! I'll lay my life they're come to speak about your preaching on the Green yesterday, Dinah, in Mr Irwine's parish! It's you must answer 'em for I'm dumb.

Dinah Dear Aunt——

Mrs Poyser To think of a niece o' mine being cause o' my husband's being turned out of his farm . . .

Dinah Nay, Aunt, you've no cause for such fears. I've strong assurance that no evil will happen to any of you from anything I've done. I didn't preach without direction.

Mrs Poyser Direction! I know what you mean by direction! When there's a bigger maggot than usual in your head, you call it "direction" and then nothing can stir you . . .

Mrs Poyser curtsys low as:

Arthur and Mr Irwine enter

Ah, Mr Irwine, Captain Donnithorne.

Mr Irwine Well, Mrs Poyser, how are you after this stormy wet morning? Our feet are quite dry, we shall not soil your beautiful floor.

Mrs Poyser Oh sir, don't mention it. Will you and the Captain please to walk into the parlour?

Arthur No indeed, thank you Mrs Poyser. I delight in your kitchen. I think it's the most charming room I know. Poyser's not home, is he?

Mrs Poyser No sir, he isn't. He's out in the fields, but——

Arthur I must come another day. I want to have a consultation with him about horses. Do you know, Mrs Poyser, I think yours is the prettiest farm on my grandfather's estate. If I were going to marry and settle I should be tempted to turn you out and do up this fine old house and turn farmer myself.

Mrs Poyser (*alarmed*) Oh sir, you wouldn't like it at all. The floors upstairs are very rotten and the rats in the cellar are beyond anything.

Arthur But there's no chance of that. I'm not likely to settle for the next twenty years, till I'm a stout gentleman of forty. (*He looks through the dairy doorway*) By the by, I've never seen your dairy; I must see your dairy, Mrs Poyser.

Mrs Poyser Indeed sir, it's not fit for you to go in, for Hetty's in the middle o' making the butter, for the churning was thrown late, and I'm quite ashamed.

Arthur Oh I've no doubt it's in capital order. Take me in . . .

Mrs Poyser (*calling*) Hetty! . . .

Mrs Poyser and Arthur exit

Mr Irwine is left to confront Dinah

Mr Irwine You're only a visitor in this neighbourhood, I think.

Dinah I come from Snowfield in Stonyshire. But my aunt invited me to stay with her for a while.

Mr Irwine Ah, I remember Snowfield. It's a dreary bleak place. They were building a cotton mill——

Dinah I work in it myself, sir.

Mr Irwine You have relations living there?

Dinah I've no other kindred now besides my Aunt Poyser.

Mr Irwine You're a Methodist, I think?

Dinah Yes.

Mr Irwine Have you been long in the habit of preaching? I understand you preached on the Green here at Hayslope last night.

Dinah I first took to the work four years since.

Mr Irwine Your society sanctions women preaching then?

Dinah It doesn't forbid them, sir, when they've a clear call to the work. It isn't for men to make channels for God's spirit, and say "Flow here, but flow not there."

Mr Irwine Tell me — I am interested — how you first came to think of preaching?

Dinah Indeed sir, I didn't think of it at all. I'm too much given to keep by myself; it seems as if I could sit silent all day long with the thought of God overflowing my soul — as the pebbles lie bathed in the Willow Brook. For thoughts are so great — aren't they, sir? They seem to lie upon us like a deep flood; and it's my besetment to forget everything about me and lose myself in thoughts that I could neither make a beginning nor ending of in words. That was my way as long as I can remember; but sometimes it seemed as if speech came to me without any will of my own and the words were given to me that came out as the tears come, because our hearts are full and we can't help it. I was suddenly called to preach and since then I've never been left in doubt about the work that was laid upon me.

There is a slight pause

Mr Irwine What did you think of your hearers last night now? Did you find them quiet, and attentive?

Dinah Very quiet, sir, but I saw no signs of any great work upon them. As different as can be from the great towns like Leeds.

Mr Irwine Why yes, our farm labourers are not so easily roused. But we have some intelligent workmen about here. I daresay you know the Bedes; Seth Bede is a Methodist.

Dinah Yes, I know Seth, and his brother, Adam, though but a little. Seth is sincere and without offence, and Adam is like the patriarch Joseph for his great skill and knowledge.

Mr Irwine Perhaps you don't know the trouble that's just happened to them? Their father was drowned in the Willow Brook last night, not far from his own door.

Dinah Ah! Their poor mother! She will mourn heavily. I must go and see if I can give her any help.

Mr Irwine We too must go. I must find Captain Donnithorne.

SCENE 5

In the Dairy

Arthur and Hetty

G. Eliot/Actor 4 Meanwhile, the dairy is certainly worth looking at.
Arthur (*stopping*) Ah!——
Hetty (*curtsying*) Sir!
Arthur ——Hetty Sorrel.

There is a slight pause

Mrs Poyser enters

Yes, Mrs Poyser, I hope you'll be ready for my twenty-first birthday feast on the thirtieth July. I shall expect you to be one of the guests who come earliest and leave latest.

Mrs Poyser bows her head

(*He watches Hetty*) Will you promise me your hand for two dances, Miss Hetty? If I don't get your promise now I shall hardly have a chance, for all the smart young farmers will take care to secure you.
Mrs Poyser Indeed sir, you're very kind to take that notice of her. And I'm sure that whenever you're pleased to dance with her, she'll be proud and thankful, if she stood still the rest o' the evening.
Arthur Oh no, that would be too cruel to all the other young fellows. But you will promise me two dances, won't you?
Hetty Yes, thank you, sir. (*She curtsys*)   ← ies?
Arthur But where is Totty today? I want to see her.
Mrs Poyser Where is my little 'un, Hetty? She came in here not long ago.
Hetty (*indifferently*) I don't know. She went into the brewhouse to Nancy, I think.

Mrs Poyser exits

There is a slight pause

Arthur And do you carry the butter to market when you've made it?
Hetty Oh no, sir. I'm not strong enough to carry it all.
Arthur No, I'm sure your pretty arms were never meant for such heavy weights. But you go out a walk sometimes these pleasant evenings, don't you? Why don't you have a walk in the Chase sometimes, now it's so green and pleasant? I hardly ever see you anywhere except at home and at church.
Hetty Aunt doesn't like me to go a-walking, only when I'm going somewhere. But I go through the Chase sometimes. When I go to see Mrs Pomfret, the lady's maid. She's teaching me the lace-mending. I'm going to tea with her tomorrow afternoon.

Mrs Poyser enters

Mrs Poyser I'm afraid that Totty seems——

❋ [INSERT]   Arthur And you must bring your little Totty, Mrs Poyser.
I want all the youngest children on the estate to be
there – all those who'll be fine young men and women
when I'm a bald old fellow.
Mrs Poyser Oh dear sir, that'll be a long time first.

Arthur But I must be going now. For I suppose the Rector will be waiting. (*He calls back as he exits*) Tell your husband I shall come and have a long talk with him soon . . .

Arthur exits as:

Mrs Poyser chases after him

G. Eliot/Actor 3 When the yard gate had closed behind the Captain and Mr Irwine, Mrs Poyser returned across the yard.

SCENE 6

In the yard

Dinah is on her way out

Mrs Poyser Why, Dinah, Mr Irwine wasn't angry then? Didn't he scold you for preaching?
Dinah No, I was quite drawn out to speak to him. He's as pleasant as the morning sunshine.
Mrs Poyser Pleasant! I should think he is . . .
Dinah But Aunt, he told me something. Thias Bede was drowned last night in the Willow Brook, and I'm thinking that the aged mother will be greatly in need of comfort. Perhaps I can be of use to her, so . . .
Mrs Poyser Dear heart, but you must have a cup o' tea first, child. As to Thias Bede, he's better out o' the way nor in — God forgi' me saying so — for he's done little this ten year but make trouble for th' old woman, and . . .

Hetty enters

Hetty I need a bunch of dock leaves; the butter's ready to pack up now.
Mrs Poyser D'you hear what's happened, Hetty?
Hetty No. How should I hear anything?
Mrs Poyser Not as you'd care much I daresay, if you did hear; you'd be perking at the glass the next minute. Adam Bede and all his kin might be drowned for all you'd care.
Hetty Adam Bede, drowned?
Dinah No, my dear, no——
Mrs Poyser (~~going~~) That man thinks a deal more of you than you deserve.— ←

~~Mrs Poyser exits~~ ←

Dinah — not Adam — Adam's father, the old man is drowned. Last night in the Willow Brook.
Hetty Oh! How dreadful . . . I must fetch the dock leaves.   and Mrs Poyser

Hetty exits .   ∧   ←

G. Eliot/Actor 3 Hetty's aunt and uncle wanted her to marry Adam.

G. Eliot/Actor 5 And if Adam had been rich she loved him well enough to marry him.

G. Eliot/Actor 4 But for the last few weeks a new influence had come over Hetty.

G. Eliot/Actor 5 Arthur Donnithorne.

SCENE 7

The way home

Mr Irwine What fascinated you so in Mrs Poyser's dairy, Arthur? Have you an interest in quarry tiles and skimming dishes?

Arthur (*after a slight pause*) No, I went to look at the pretty butter maker, Hetty Sorrel. If I were an artist I'd paint her. She has the most charming phiz imaginable.

Mr Irwine Well, I've no objection to your contemplating Hetty in an artistic light, but I mustn't have you filling her little noddle with the notion that she's attractive to fine gentlemen, or you'll spoil her for a poor man's wife.

SCENE 8

The Bedes' cottage

G. Eliot/Actor 2 At the Bedes' cottage Adam rose very early the next morning.

Adam prepares for work on his father's coffin

He couldn't help saying to himself that, with his father's death, and by hard work, his circumstances might now be brought into a shape that would allow him to think of marrying.

Adam (*to himself*) But does Hetty love me in return? I've never dared to ask her. Ah, Hetty . . . (*He snaps himself out of it*) A pretty building I'm making—I'm up in the garret already, and haven't so much as dug the foundations! (*Suddenly he looks up*) Who's that?

G. Eliot/Actor 5 There was a light footstep on the stairs . . .

Adam As if it could be Hetty!

Dinah enters

Dinah How do you do, Adam Bede.

There is a pause. They take each other in slowly

G. Eliot/Actor 2 It was like dreaming of the sunshine and awakening in the moonlight.

Adam It's Dinah, isn't it? I was quite taken by surprise. You must have come last night to see my mother in her trouble.

Dinah Yes.
Adam I was in bed early.

Dinah nods

I hope my mother was thankful to have you.
Dinah Yes, she seemed greatly comforted after a while, and she's had a good deal of rest in the night by times. She's fast asleep now.
Adam Who was it took the news to the Hall Farm?
Dinah Mr Irwine, the clergyman. They'll look for you there as soon as you've got time to go, for there's nobody round that hearth but what's glad to see you. (*She has Hetty in mind*)
Adam (*pleased*) Ah! Thank you. But you won't be there yourself any longer?
Dinah No, I go back to Snowfield on Saturday. But I can stay here today if your mother would like me; her heart seemed inclined towards me last night.
Adam Ah, if Mother takes to people at the beginning, she's sure to get fond of them. But she's a strange way of not liking young women. (*Smiling*) Though to be sure, her not liking other young women is no reason why she shouldn't like you.

Seth Bede enters and stands looking at them for a moment. An unconscious triangle

Dinah (*turning to him*) Seth Bede, I won't say farewell. I shall see you again when you come home from work.
Seth Thank you, Dinah. I should like to walk back to Hall Farm with you this evening. It'll perhaps be the last time.
Dinah You'll have peace in your mind today, Seth, for your tenderness towards your mother.

Dinah exits

Adam I don't wonder at thee for loving her, Seth. She's got a face like a lily.
Seth (*first confession*) Ay, Addy, I do love her. But she doesn't love me, lad, only as one child o' God loves another. She'll never love any man as a husband — that's my belief.
Adam (*to comfort*) Nay lad, there's no telling. She's made out of stuff with a finer grain than most o' the women. I can see that clear enough. But if she's better than they are in other things, I canna think she'll fall short of 'em in loving. (*He goes back to work*)

SCENE 9

The Grove — evening light

Arthur comes to the centre of the stage. His coat is brought to him

G. Eliot/Actor 4 Captain Arthur Donnithorne was nothing if not good-natured.

G. Eliot/Actor 1 Deeds of kindness were as easy to him as a bad habit.

G. Eliot/Actor 6 He was but twenty-one.

Arthur (*singing to himself cheerfully*)

> "When the heart of a man is oppressed with cares
> The mist is dispelled when a woman appears . . ."

(*He hums quietly*)

G. Eliot/Actor 2 And we don't enquire too closely into character in the case of a handsome, generous young fellow, who, if he should unfortunately break a man's legs in his rash driving, will be able to pension him handsomely.

G. Eliot/Actor 5 Or, if he should happen to spoil a woman's existence for her, will make it up to her with expensive bon-bons — packed up and directed by his own hand.

G. Eliot/Actor 6 The chances are that he will go through life without scandalising anyone.

Arthur I'll amuse myself by seeing Hetty today simply to remove any false impression and then get rid of the whole thing from my mind. It's all Irwine's fault. If he'd said nothing I shouldn't have thought . . . (*He listens and waits expectantly*)

Hetty comes in and stops

They look at each other

You're quite right to choose this way through the Chase. The Grove here is so much prettier, as well as shorter.

Hetty Yes, sir.

Arthur Do you come every week to see Mrs Pomfret?

Hetty Yes sir, every Thursday.

Arthur And she's teaching you something, is she?

Hetty Yes sir, the lace-mending as she's learnt abroad, and the stocking mending . . . (*pause*) and she teaches me cutting-out too.

Arthur What, are you going to be a lady's maid?

Hetty I should like to be one, very much indeed.

Arthur I mustn't keep you now, else I should like to show you my retreat, The Hermitage. Did you ever see it?

Hetty No sir.

Arthur (*pointing*) This is where we turn up to it. (*After a slight pause*) But we mustn't go now. I'll show it to you some other time if you'd like to see it.

Hetty Yes, please, sir.

Arthur (*after a slight pause*) Do you always come back this way in the evening, or are you afraid to come so lonely a road?

Hetty Oh no sir, it's so light now in the evening. But my aunt would be angry with me if I didn't get home before nine.

Arthur Perhaps Craig, the gardener, comes to take care of you?

Hetty I'm sure he doesn't; I'm sure he never did; I wouldn't let him; I don't like him. (*She begins to cry*)

Arthur (*putting his arms round her*) Why Hetty, what makes you cry? I didn't mean to vex you. I wouldn't vex you for the world, you little blossom. Come, don't cry; look at me, else I think you won't forgive me.

They look at each other. Very, very slowly, they kiss. She drops her basket. They stoop to pick things up. Arthur looks at his watch

I've been hindering you. I mustn't keep you any longer now. You'll be expected at home. (*He presses her hand*) Trot along. Goodbye.

Hetty exits reluctantly

After a pause, Arthur recovers his composure

Arthur I'm getting in love with her. We'll get too fond of each other if I go on. No gentleman can marry a farmer's niece. There must be an end to the whole thing at once. It's too foolish. I mustn't see her alone again. (*After a slight pause*) I must see her again, simply to remove any false impression from her mind . . . If only circumstances were different . . . To put my arm round her again, to look into her sweet face . . . (*He becomes resolved*) No, I must go and tell Irwine everything. I'll walk to Broxton Rectory the first thing tomorrow.

SCENE 10

Hall Farm

The two bedrooms: A divided stage

G. Eliot/Actor 1 At the Hall Farm, Hetty and Dinah both slept upstairs——
G. Eliot/Actor 5 —in bedrooms adjoining each other.

Dinah sits on her bed looking out of the window — she watches the moonlight

Hetty sits on her bed looking into the mirror — she lets her hair down

G. Eliot/Actor 1 Dinah delighted in her bedroom window. Her heart was very full, for there was to be only one more night on which she would look out on those fields for a long time to come.
Dinah (*praying*) And all those dear people . . . Seth and Adam . . . Lisbeth Bede . . . and my aunt and uncle . . . and . . . Hetty . . . (*She closes her eyes*)

There is a stillness, which is broken by Hetty

Hetty I am very pretty—prettier than any of the ladies I've ever seen visiting at the Chase. Captain Donnithorne won't like me to go on doing work. He'll like to see me in nice stockings, perhaps with silk clocks to 'em. He must love me very much—no-one else has ever put his arms round me and kissed me in that way. He'll want to marry me—make a lady of me—Oh!—But how else can it be? He'll marry me quite secretly. Nobody'll find out for a long time after and then it'll be no use being angry. I don't know how, but—he'll know. He's a great gentleman and can have his way in everything. Perhaps some day I'll be a grand lady and

ride in a coach and dress for dinner in a brocaded silk . . . Perhaps Mary
Burge and everybody will see me . . . (*She breaks off, and walks up and
down, carrying a hand mirror*)

G. Eliot/Actor 2 Adam was sure that Hetty's love, wherever she gave it,
would be the most precious thing a man could possess on earth.

G. Eliot/Actor 3 But one begins to suspect that there is no direct correlation
between long eyelashes and depth of soul.

G. Eliot/Actor 4 Arthur was sure that she was a dear, affectionate good little
thing. He probably imagined himself being virtuously tender to her,
because the poor thing is so clingingly fond of him.

G. Eliot/Actor 6 But people who love downy peaches are not apt to think
of the stone.

Suddenly, Hetty drops the mirror

Dinah opens her eyes and listens ~~at the door to Hetty's room~~. She opens the *goes to the
bible ~~and opens it~~. She reads for a moment and then makes a decision. She taps
at Hetty's door*

Dinah Hetty? (*Slight pause*) Will you let me come in?

Hetty quickly hides her mirror and other signs of vanity

Hetty Yes, come in.

Dinah enters

Dinah I knew you weren't in bed, I heard you moving. I wanted to speak
to you. Shall I sit while you do up your hair?

Hetty Oh, yes. (*She starts to do her hair with an air of excessive indifference*)

There is a pause while Dinah sits

Dinah Hetty, it's been borne in upon my mind tonight that you may some
day be in trouble. I want to tell you that if ever you are and need a friend
that will always feel for you and love you, you've got that friend in me.
If you come to me, or send for me, I'll never forget this night and the
words I'm speaking now.

Hetty turns, frightened

Will you remember it, Hetty?

Hetty Yes, but why should you think I shall be in trouble? Do you know
of anything?

Dinah (*leaning forward and taking Hetty's hands*) Trouble comes to us all in
this life. We set our hearts on things which it isn't God's will for us to
have, and then we go sorrowing. The people we love are taken from us and
we can joy in nothing because they are not with us; we go astray and do
wrong and bring ourselves into trouble with our fellow men. There is no
man or woman born into this world to whom some of these trials don't
fall — so I feel some of them must happen to you.

Hetty is fearful. She beings to cry

Oh, Hetty, won't you unburden your heart to me? Yes, Hetty, speak to
me.

Hetty suddenly pushes her away

Hetty Don't talk to me so, Dinah. Why do you come to frighten me? I've never done anything to you! . . . (*Violently*) Why can't you let me be!

Dinah (*sorry she has spoken*) . . . I won't hinder you any longer. You're tired. Good-night! (*She goes back to her room*).

They each stand for a moment by their beds, upset. Then they each go down on their knees; Hetty to cry bitterly, Dinah to pray

G. Eliot/Actor 6 Hetty couldn't unburden her heart to Dinah . . .

SCENE 11

The road to the Rectory—bright sunlight

G. Eliot/Actor 6 However, Arthur Donnithorne has a sincere determination to open his heart to the Rector.

G. Eliot/Actor 4 And the swirling sound of the scythe as he passes the meadow is all the pleasanter to him because of this earnest purpose.

G. Eliot/Actor 6 On the road to the Rectory, he saw Adam Bede.

Arthur Adam!

They shake hands warmly

Well, Adam, how are you? I would swear to your shoulders a long way off. Just the same only broader, as when you used to carry me on them! Do you remember?

Adam Ah, sir, I remember. It 'ud be a poor look-out if folks didn't remember what they did and said when they were lads. We should think no more about old friends than we do about new 'uns then.

Arthur Are you going to the Rectory too?

Adam (*pointing another way*) No, sir, I'm going to see about Bradwell's barn. They're afraid of the roof pushing the walls out, and I'm going to see what can be done with it, before they send the workmen.

Arthur Why, Burge trusts almost everything to you now, Adam, doesn't he? I should think he'll make you his partner soon. If you and Mary Burge . . .

Adam Nay, sir, a foreman, if he delights in his work, will do his business as well as a partner.

Arthur When's your father to be buried?

Adam On Sunday, sir. I shall be glad when it's over, for I think my mother'll perhaps get easier then. It cuts me sadly to see the grief of old people—they've no way of working it off.

Arthur Ah, you've had a good deal of trouble in your life, Adam. I don't think you've ever been harebrained and lighthearted like other youngsters.

Adam (*shrugging*) If we've men's feelings, I reckon we must have men's troubles. We can't be like the birds. I've allays had health and strength and I count it a great thing as I've had Bartle Massey's night school to go to. He's helped me to knowledge I could never ha' got by myself.

Arthur What a rare fellow you are Adam. (*He looks at him*) I could hit out better than most men at Oxford and yet I believe you'd knock me into next week if I were to have a battle with you.

Adam (*grinning*) God forbid I should ever do that sir!

Arthur I should think you never have any struggles within yourself. I mean first making up your mind that you won't do a thing, and then doing it after all?

Adam Well, no — not when I'd made my mind up that a thing was wrong. I think my fault lies the other way. When I've said a thing — if it's only to myself, it's hard for me to go back.

Arthur Yes, you've got an iron will. But however strong a man's resolution may be, it costs him something to carry it out now and then. We may determine not to gather any cherries, but we can't prevent our mouths from watering.

Adam That's true, sir, but there's a deal we must do without. It's no good looking on life as if it was Treddleston fair. But you know better than I do.

Arthur I'm not so sure. You've had four to five years of experience more than I've had and I think your life has been a better school to you than college has been to me.

Adam Bartle Massey says college mostly makes people like bladders — good for nothing but t' hold the stuff as is poured into 'em. But he's got a tongue like a sharp blade, Bartle has. But I must bid you good-morning, sir, as you're going to the Rectory.

Arthur Ah yes, goodbye.

They go their separate ways

SCENE 12

The Rectory

Mr Irwine settles himself in a chair with a book

G. Eliot/Actor 6 The Reverend Mr Irwine was Rector of Broxton and Vicar of Hayslope. A pluralist, and a man of no very lofty aims.

Arthur Mr Irwine.

→ **Mr Irwine** (*delightedly*) Why, this is like the old days, Arthur, you haven't been to breakfast with me these five years!

Arthur It was a tempting morning. I used to enjoy it so, when I was reading with you.

Mr Irwine I like breakfast time better than any other moment in the day. I always have a favourite book by me and regularly every morning it seems to me as if I should certainly become studious again. But presently I've got my "justicing" and the day goes on, and I'm always the same lazy fellow before evening sets in. If you'd stuck to your books well, you rascal, I should have a pleasanter prospect before me.

→ *had* ^

Arthur But I don't think a knowledge of the classics is a pressing want to

a country gentleman; as far as I can see he'd much better have a knowledge of manures. My grandfather will never let me have any power while
he lives, but there's nothing I should like better than to set improvements
on foot and gallop about and overlook them. I should like to know all the
labourers and see them touching their hats to me with a look of goodwill.

Mr Irwine Bravo Arthur! And you'll want a portly Rector to complete the
picture and take his tithe of all the respect you get. Only I'm not sure that
men are the fondest of them who try to be useful to them. You must make
it quite clear to your mind which you are most bent upon, old boy—
popularity or usefulness.

Arthur Oh, I don't believe there's anything you can't prevail on people to
do with kindness. If fair allowances were made to them and their buildings
attended to, one could persuade them to farm on a better plan.

Mr Irwine Then mind you fall in love in the right place and don't get a wife
who will drain your purse. (*After a slight pause*) My mother and I have
a little discussion about you sometimes: she says "I'll never risk a single
prophecy on Arthur till I see the woman he falls in love with." She thinks
your lady-love will rule you as the moon rules the tides. But I feel bound
to stand up for you, as my pupil you know. And I maintain that you're
not of that watery quality. So mind you don't disgrace my judgement.

Arthur Mm. But I think it's hardly an argument against a man's general
strength of character that he should be apt to be mastered by love. A fine
constitution doesn't insure one against smallpox. A man may be very firm
in other matters and yet be under a sort of witchery from a woman.

Mr Irwine Yes, but if you detect the disease at an early stage, and try change
of air, there's every chance of a complete escape.

Arthur You don't think a man who struggles against a temptation into
which he falls at last, is as bad as the man who never struggles at all.

Mr Irwine No, my boy, I pity him in proportion to his struggles. But
consequences are unpitying . . . and they are hardly ever confined to
ourselves. It's best to fix our minds on that certainty, instead of considering what may be the elements of excuse for us. But I never knew you so
inclined for moral discussion, Arthur. Is there some danger of your own
you are considering in this philosophical general way?

There is a pause

Arthur (*indifferently*) Oh no, no danger. Only there are little incidents now
and then that set one speculating on what might happen in the
future . . . I think I might take myself off to Eagledale for a few days'
fishing . . .

G. Eliot/Actor 4 It wasn't after all a thing to make a fuss about. What could
Irwine do for him that he couldn't do for himself?

G. Eliot/Actor 6 Or was it secretly the fear that he might hereafter find
having made a confession to the Rector a serious annoyance?

There is a slight pause

G. Eliot/Actor 4 The human soul is a very complex thing.

SCENE 13

The Church

The community gathers around the coffin

G. Eliot/Actor 6 That Sunday, at Thias Bede's funeral, all of Hayslope was at Church.

G. Eliot/Actor 4 But for Arthur, who had gone to Eagledale.

Mr Irwine Let us pray.

All kneel

G. Eliot/Actor 3 Lisbeth cried less today than she had done any day since her husband's death; along with all her grief there was mixed an unusual sense of her own importance in having a "burial".

G. Eliot/Actor 2 Adam felt sorrow because the chief source of his past trouble and vexation was forever gone out of his reach. But he thought "There's no real making amends in this world, anymore nor you can mend a wrong subtraction by doing your addition right."

Hetty starts to cry. People begin to notice. Adam looks at her with love

G. Eliot/Actor 3 Mrs Poyser thought "We shall all on us be dead some time I reckon. It's but little good you'll do a-watering last year's crop."

G. Eliot/Actor 5 But Hetty, in this moment of chill disappointment and anger at Arthur's absence, yet looked towards the possibility of being with him again with that eager yearning which one may call the "growing pain" of passion.

SCENE 14

The Bedes' Cottage

G. Eliot/Actor 2 The next day at the Bedes' cottage, Adam had changed his clothes and was ready to go out.

Lisbeth sits in her chair

Lisbeth What's thee got thy Sunday cloose on for on a Monday? Thee artna going to Bartle Massey's school i' thy best coat?

Adam No, Mother. I'm going to the Hall Farm, but mayhap I may go on to see Mr Massey after, so thee mustna wonder if I'm a bit late. Seth 'ull be home in half an hour, so thee wotna mind.

Lisbeth Eh and what's thee got thy best cloose on for to go to th' Hall Farm. The Poyser folks see'd thee in 'em at the burial yesterday I warrant . . .

Adam Goodbye, Mother, I can't stay.

Lisbeth (*stopping him as he goes*) Nay, my lad, thee wotna go away angered wi' thy mother an' her got nought to do but to sit by hersen and think o' thee?

Adam Nay, nay, Mother, I'm not angered. But I wish, for thy own sake, thee'd be more contented to let me do what I've made up my mind to do. I'll never be no other than a good son to thee as long as we live. But a man has other feelings besides what he owes to his father and mother; and thee must make up thy mind, as I'll not give way to thee where I've a right to do what I like. So let's have no more words about it.

There is a moment

Lisbeth Eh, an' who likes to see thee i' thy best cloose better nor thy mother? An' when thee'st got thy face washed as clean as the smooth white pibble, an' thy hair combed so nice an' thy eyes a-sparklin — what else is there as thy old mother should like to look at half so well? I'll ne'er plague thee no moor about'n.
Adam Well, well. Goodbye, Mother.

He kisses her and goes

Lisbeth Eh, he'll be tellin' me as he's goin' to bring Hetty home one o' these days; an' she'll be missus o'er me an I mun look on, belike, while she uses the blue edged platters, and breaks 'em mayhap. That's what comes o' marr'in young wenches. I war gone thirty, an' th' feyther too, afore we war married, an' young enough too. She'll be a poor dratchell by then she's thirty, a-marr'in an' a-that'n, afore her teeth's all come . . .

SCENE 15

The Hall Farm garden

Evening light

G. Eliot/Actor 2 When Adam reached the Hall Farm, Mrs Poyser gave him some whey to drink and then sent him into the kitchen garden, where Hetty was gathering redcurrants.

Adam enters with a rose in his buttonhole

Hetty suddenly becomes aware of him and turns

Hetty (*confused; she drops her basket*) Oh!
Adam I frightened you.
Hetty I shall soon ha' done now.
Adam I'll help you.

But they stay looking at each other

G. Eliot/Actor 6 It was to Adam the time that a man can least forget in afterlife — the time when he believes that the first woman he has ever loved betrays by a slight something that she is at least beginning to love him in return.
G. Eliot/Actor 2 Hetty bending over the red bunches, the evening sunbeams stealing through the apple trees, his own emotion as he looked at her and

believed she was thinking of him and there was no need for them to talk; Adam remembered it all to the last moment of his life.

G. Eliot/Actor 1 And Hetty? She had been absorbed as usual in thinking about Arthur's possible return from Eagledale — the sound of any man's footstep would have affected her in the same way.

G. Eliot/Actor 5 Yet in the anxieties and fears of her first passion, there was something soothing to her in Adam's tenderness; she wanted to be treated lovingly.

G. Eliot/Actor 1 She was not the first woman who had behaved more gently to the man who loved her in vain, because she had herself begun to love another.

Hetty Oh that'll do. Aunt wants me to leave some on the trees. (*She sits*)

Adam It's well I came to carry the basket, for it 'ud ha' been too heavy for your little arms.

Hetty No, I could ha' carried it.

Adam (*smiling*) Oh, I daresay, and been as long getting to the house as an ant carrying a caterpillar. Have you ever seen that?

Hetty No.

Adam I used to watch 'em often when I was a lad.

There is a pause

Hetty Have you ever been to Eagledale?

Adam Yes, ten years ago as a lad, I went with Father to see about some work there. It's a wonderful sight, rocks and caves such as you never saw in your life.

Hetty How long did it take to get there?

Adam Why, it took us the best part o' two days' walking. But the Captain 'ud get there in nine or ten hours I'd be bound, he's such a rider. And I shouldn't wonder if he's back again tomorrow; he's too active to rest long in that lonely place, all by himself.

Hetty leans forward with interest

I wish he'd got th' estate in his hands — that 'ud be the right thing for him — he's got better notions o' things than many a man twice his age. He spoke very handsome to me th' other day about lending me money to set up i' business, and if things came round that way, I'd rather be beholding to him nor to any man i' the world. (*Slight pause*) The roses are pretty now. But I've got the prettiest. See! Stick it in your frock and then you can put it in water after.

Hetty takes it, smiling, and sticks it over her ear

Ah, that's like the ladies in the picture at the Chase; they've mostly got flowers or gold things in their hair. But if a woman's young and pretty, I think you can see her good looks all the better for her being plain dressed. Why, Dinah looks very nice for all she wears such a plain cap. It seems to me a woman's face doesn't want flowers; it's almost like a flower itself. I'm sure yours is.

Hetty Oh, very well. (*She takes the rose out*) I'll put one o' Dinah's caps on when we go in. She left one behind.

Adam Nay, nay, I don't want you to wear a Methodist cap, it fits her face somehow, as th' acorn cup fits th' acorn, but you've another sort of face. I'd have you just as you are now without anything t'interfere with your own looks.

They look at each other. Adam decides to speak

Adam Hetty . . .
Hetty (*quickly*) Shall we take in the currants now?
Adam (*rising*) Let me give you my arm to lean on.

Mr and Mrs Poyser enter, with their arms around each other

Mr Poyser Well, Adam, I'm glad to see ye.
Adam Mr Poyser.
Mr Poyser What, ye've been helping Hetty to gather the currants, eh? (*He laughs*) Why it's pretty near a three-week since y' had your supper wi' us and the missus has got one of her rare stuffed chines.
Mrs Poyser Well, Adam, I'm glad ye're come.
Mr Poyser Come in and sit ye down. Sit ye down.
G. Eliot/Actor 2 So Adam entered the warm houseplace, where the supper was being laid on the oak table.
G. Eliot/Actor 3 That evening, after a fine family supper, when Adam had left to go on to see Bartle Massey,

Adam exits

Mr Poyser said:
Mr Poyser Ye'll not find many men o' six and twenty as 'ull do to put i' the shafts wi' him. If you can catch Adam for a husband, Hetty, you'll ride i' your own spring-cart some day, I'll be your warrant.
G. Eliot/Actor 5 But to ride in a spring-cart seemed a very miserable lot to Hetty now.

SCENE 16

The Night School
There is lamplight, Bartle Massey is at the blackboard. Bill a workman sits trying to read

G. Eliot/Actor 6 Bartle Massey's night school was drawing to its end.
G. Eliot/Actor 2 It was a familiar scene to Adam.
Bill The sticks . . . are . . . d . . . dog? Eh, Mr Massey . . .
Bartle Massey Nay, Bill, nay. Begin that again, and then perhaps it'll come to you what d, r, y, spells. It's the same lesson you read last week, you know.
Bill The letters are so uncommon alike, there's no way of tellin' 'em one from another.

Bartle Massey Now, you see, you don't do this thing a bit better than you
did a fortnight ago, and I'll tell you what's the reason. You think knowledge is to be got cheap — you'll come and pay Bartle Massey sixpence a
week, and he'll make you clever at figures without your taking any
trouble. But I'll have nobody in my night school that doesn't strive to
learn what he comes to learn as hard as if he was striving to get out of a
dark hole into broad daylight. So never come to me again if you can't
show that you've been working with your own head, instead of thinking
you can pay for mine to work for you. That's the last word I've got to say
to you.

Bill rises abashed

Bill Good-night, Mr Massey.
Bartle Massey Good-night, Bill.

Bill exits

Well, Adam. You've had a rough bit o' road to get over since I saw you
— a rough bit o' road. But I'm in hopes there are better times coming. (*He
brings out some bread rolls*) Now then my boy, draw up, draw up. No man
can be wise on an empty stomach.
Adam I'll look on. I've been at the Hall Farm, and they always have their
supper betimes, you know. They don't keep your late hours.
Bartle Massey It's a house I seldom go into. Too many women in the house
for me. I hate the sound of women's voices — they're always either a-buzz
or a-squeak. Will you take some ale, my boy?
Adam Nay, Mr Massey, don't be so hard on the creatures God has made
to be companions for us. A working man 'ud be badly off without a wife
to see to the house and make things comfortable, and——
Bartle Massey Nonsense. It's the silliest lie a sensible man like you ever
believed to say a woman makes a house comfortable. It's a story got up
because the women are there, and something must be found for them to
do. I tell you there isn't a thing under the sun that needs to be done at all,
but what a man can do better than a woman, unless it's bearing children,
and they do that in a poor makeshift way — it had better ha' been left to
the men — it had better ha' been left to the men.

There is a slight pause
Adam. But Mr Massey —
Bartle Massey (*He starts again even more violently*) It's an impious opinion to say a
woman's a blessing to a man — you might as well say adders and wasps
and wild hogs are a blessing. Man should keep as clear of women as he
can in this life and hope to get quit of 'em forever in another, and hope
to get quit of 'em forever in another. But tell me, have you any particular
news today?   (*Pause*)
Adam No. What 'ud that be?
Bartle Massey You know the Captain once said, in plenty of people's
hearing that he'd make you manager of his woods tomorrow if he'd the
power. Well, it seems there's a fair opportunity for making a change. The

Captain's coming of age now and it's to be expected he'll have a little more voice in things.

Adam Nay, there's not much likelihood the old squire 'ud ever consent t'employ me. He thinks me over-proud. If the Captain was really master o' the estate, it 'ud be different. He's got a conscience and a will to do right.

Bartle Massey Well, well my boy, if good luck knocks at your door, don't tell it to be gone about its business, that's all. Where's the use of all the time I've spent in teaching you writing and mapping and mensuration if you're not to get forward in the world, and show folks there's some advantage in having a head on your shoulders instead of a turnip.

Adam Well I'll think o' what you've been saying, but till then I've got nothing to do but to trust to my own hands. I'm turning over a little plan for Seth and me to go into the cabinet making a bit by ourselves, and win an extra pound or two in that way and then I could think of marrying and . . .

Bartle Massey Marryin'?! (*He is about to explode*) Marryin'!!

There is a slight pause

Adam But it's getting late — it'll be pretty near eleven before I'm at home and Mother may happen to lie awake — so . . . I'll bid you good-night.

Bartle Massey Well, well.

He sees him to the door

Come to the music o' Friday night, if you can, my boy.

Adam Ay, ay.

Adam exits

Bartle Massey Ay, ay. (*Looking after him*) There you go stalking along — stalking along. But you wouldn't have been what you are if you hadn't had a bit of old lame Bartle inside you.

SCENE 17

The birthday feast

Bright sunlight

G. Eliot/Actor 4 More than a month passed and then the thirtieth of July was come, the day of Arthur's twenty-first birthday feast.

G. Eliot/Actor 3 All Broxton and Hayslope were at the Chase, to make merry there in honour of th' heir to the estate.

People pass by busily preparing for the feast. There is a sense of excitement

Arthur Upon my word these cloisters will make a delightful dining-room on a hot day.

Mr Irwine Yes, and if the people get a good dinner and a moderate quantity of ale in the middle of the day, they'll be able to enjoy the games and dancing as the day cools. You can't hinder some of them from getting too much towards evening, but drunkenness and darkness go better together than drunkenness and daylight.

Arthur Well, I hope there won't be too much of it! (*He looks up*) If I'm ever master here I shall do up the gallery in first rate style. Come and see the dinner tables for the large tenants. And I'll tell you something that will surprise you. My grandfather has come round after all.

Mr Irwine (*as they start to go*) What, about Adam?

Arthur Yes. I thought it was hopeless, but yesterday . . .

Mr Irwine and Arthur exit as:

Mrs Poyser and Hetty enter

Mrs Poyser Why, the Chase is like a fair already. I should ha' thought there wasna so many people i' the two parishes. Massy on us, how hot it is out o' the shade. Where's my littl'un, Hetty?

Hetty goes one way looking for Arthur, Mrs Poyser goes another, chasing after Totty

Come here, Totty, else your little face 'ull be burnt to a scratchin'.

Mr Poyser enters

Mr Poyser Stop a bit, stop a bit. There's th' waggin coming wi' th' old folks in't. It'll be such a sight as wonna come o'er again . . .

Mr Poyser exits as:

Adam enters with Seth

Adam . . . to dine upstairs. The Captain wishes it particular, Seth lad. I could sit with the Poysers. But I don't like sitting up above thee and Mother as if I was better than my own flesh and blood. Thee't not take it unkind, I hope?

Seth Nay lad, thy honour's our honour. Mother 'ull be fine and joyful about it. Let's go and tell her. It's nothing but what's right.

As they move on perhaps there is the sound of musicians warming up

Mary, Bill and Bartle Massey enter, and a table is carried on

Mary Nay, Bill, it's allays been the oldest tenant that holds the top seat.

Bill I should ha' thought, Mary Burge, the tenant with the most land had the best right, more nor th' oldest.

Mary Eh, here's Mr Massey. The schoolmaster ought to be able to tell you what's right. Who's to sit at top o' table, Mr Massey?

Bartle Massey Why the broadest man, and then he won't take up other folks' room.

There is laughter as people bring chairs and mugs

Hetty Oh dear, Aunt, I wish you'd speak to Totty. She keeps putting her legs up so and messing my frock.

Mrs Poyser What's the matter wi' the child? She can niver please you.

Mary And we'll sing "Over the hills and far away" after dinner, wonna we Bill, and then we'll dance.

Bill Peeh! It's not to be named besides o' the Scotch tunes.

Bartle Massey The Scotch tunes! They're fit for nothing but to frighten the birds with.

Bill Yes, there's folks as find pleasure in undervalleying what they know little about.

Bill exits. Bartle Massey goes after him

Bartle Massey Why the Scotch tunes are just like a nagging woman. They go on over and over again and never come to a reasonable end.

Mrs Poyser, Adam, Hetty and Mary gather round the table

Mary Who's to sit at top o' table? Who's the broadest man then?

Mr Poyser enters

All (*laughing*) Mr Poyser, Mr Poyser!

He is led to the top of the table. They all sit talking at once

Arthur enters after a ~~time~~ moment

They all stand respectfully

Arthur (*motioning them to sit down*) My grandfather and I hope all our friends here will have enjoyed their dinner and find my birthday ale good. I've come to taste it with you!

All turn to Mr Poyser, with whispers of "Mr Poyser, go on now"

Mr Poyser (*standing*) Captain. My neighbours have put it upo' me to speak for 'em today, for where folks think pretty much alike, one spokesman's as good as a score. We've pretty well all on us known you when you war a little 'un, an' we've niver known anything on you but was good an' honourable. We look forrard to your being our landlord for we b'lieve you mean to do right by everybody, an' 'ull make no man's bread bitter to him if you can help it.

Arthur looks a little uncomfortable

That's what I mean an' that's what we all mean; an' when a man's said what he means, he'd better stop, for th' ale 'ull be none the better for stannin'. (*Pause*) I've no more to say as concerns the present time, an' so we'll drink our young Squire's health.

All shout and toast "Captain Donnithorne"

Arthur I thank you all, my good friends and neighbours. In the course of things we may expect, if I live, I shall one day or other be your landlord.

All cheer

It will be my first desire to afford my tenants all the encouragement a landlord can give them in improving their land. It'll be my wish to be looked on by all my deserving tenants as their best friend, and nothing would make me so happy as to be able to respect every man on the estate, and be respected by him in turn. But the pleasure I feel wouldn't be perfect if we didn't drink to the health of my grandfather who has filled the place of both parents to me. I will say no more until you have joined me in drinking his health.

There is only polite applause. They drink to "Squire Donnithorne"

I thank you. And now I think there can be no man here who hasn't a high regard for my friend, Adam Bede. I'm proud to say that I was very fond of Adam when I was a little boy, and I've never lost my old feeling for him. It's been my wish that he should have the management of the woods on the estate, which happen to be very valuable. And I'm happy to tell you that it is my grandfather's wish too, and it's now settled that Adam shall manage the woods. I hope you'll join me in drinking his health — Adam Bede!

There are cheers and great enthusiasm

Mr Poyser And may he live to have sons as faithful and clever as himself!
Arthur Hear, hear!
Adam (*rising*) I'll only say that I take it at Captain Donnithorne's desire. I'd wish for no better lot than to work under him and to know that I was taking care of his interests. For I believe he's one o' those gentlemen as wishes to do the right things, and to leave the world a bit better than he found it. There's no occasion for me to say anymore about what I feel towards him. I hope to show it through the rest o' my life in my actions.

All cheer and sing "For he's a jolly good fellow"

Arthur And now, the dancing!

Cheering as tables are cleared for dancing

Hetty and Arthur meet

Hetty Sir?

Arthur looks around, he shakes his head and moves away

   (*Calling after him*) Sir?
Mr Poyser Why, Adam, you're going to have a bit o' fun, I hope. And here's Hetty has promised no end o' partners, an' I've just been askin' her if she'd agreed to dance wi' you, an' she says no.
Adam Well, I didn't think o'dancing tonight, since it's not a five week since my father . . . (*He looks at Hetty and is tempted*)
Mr Poyser Nonsense. Why, everybody's goin' to dance tonight — all but

the old Squire. You canna for shame stand still, Adam, and you a fine young fellow and can dance as well as anybody.

Mrs Poyser Nay, it 'ud be unbecomin' not to dance!

Adam Then, if Hetty u'll dance with me . . .

Arthur (*approaching*) I'm come to request the favour of the first dance.

There is silence

Your hand, Mrs Poyser.

A country dance begins. Arthur starts the dance with Mrs Poyser, Hetty with Adam but the partners change—rhythmic stamping. When Hetty and Adam are together again, all freeze

Adam If a strong arm to work for her, and a heart to love her could do it, I'd make her life a happy 'un.

The dance continues—When Hetty and Arthur are together, all freeze

Arthur She will look like that when I tell her we must part, and I'll never be able to bear it. I'll give way again.

The dance finishes

As Hetty leaves the floor with Adam, her necklace falls

Hetty Oh my locket! My locket!

Adam (*picking it up and turning it over in his hand*) It isn't hurt.

Hetty Oh, it doesn't matter.

Adam Not matter?

Hetty I don't mind about it.

Adam You seemed frightened. Here. (*He gives it back to her*) Hetty . . .?

But she is gone

(*He turns away*) Perhaps she's bought the locket for herself . . . Perhaps she's ashamed because she knows I disapprove of finery . . . Yes, probably . . .

Adam exits

G. Eliot/Actor 1 Adam wove for himself an ingenious web of probabilities. It's the surest screen a man can place between himself and the truth.

Arthur enters with Hetty

Arthur (*quietly*) I shall be in the Grove the day after tomorrow at seven. Come as early as you can. (*To the audience*) My last weakness.

G. Eliot/Actor 6 A man never lies with a more delicious langour under the influence of passion than when he has persuaded himself that he shall subdue it tomorrow.

The dance strikes up merrily again. Arthur is with Hetty

The others watch

Mr Poyser (*above the dance; to everyone*) It'll serve you to talk on, Hetty, when you're an old woman — how you danced wi' the young squire the day he came o' age.

The dance ends with claps and cheers

G. Eliot/Actor 2 But three weeks after the birthday feast Adam's hopes were once more buoyant about Hetty. He had never mentioned the locket to her again, and she had seemed to make an effort to behave more kindly to him.

G. Eliot/Actor 6 Adam had been working late on some planned rebuilding at the Chase Farm and the sun was on the point of setting. He thought he might shorten his way home by striking through the Grove.

SCENE 18

The Grove

Evening light. Adam turns to look up

G. Eliot/Actor 2 He couldn't help pausing to look at a curious large beech tree.

Arthur and Hetty enter — they don't see Adam

G. Eliot/Actor 1 For the rest of his life he remembered that moment when he was calmly examining the beech, as a man remembers his last glimpse of the home where his youth was passed, before the road turned and he saw it no more.

He turns to see Arthur kissing Hetty passionately. They see Adam

Hetty exits running

While Arthur turns towards Adam

Arthur (~~laughing suddenly~~) Well, Adam, you've been looking at the fine old beeches, eh? They're not for cutting though! (*Pause*) I overtook little Hetty Sorrel as I was coming to my den, The Hermitage there. (*He points*) She oughtn't to come home this way so late — so I took care of her to the gate and asked for a kiss for my pains. But I must get back now (*laughing and looking at his shoes*) — this road is confoundedly damp. Good-night, Adam. Oh, I'm going back to my regiment tomorrow you know — I shall see you before I go . . . (*He starts to go*)

Adam Stop a bit, sir.

Arthur What do you mean?

Adam You don't deceive me. This is not the first time you've met Hetty in this Grove and this is not the first time you've kissed her.

There is a pause

Arthur Well, what then?

Adam You know as well as I do what it's to lead to when a gentleman like you kisses and makes love to a young woman like Hetty, and gives her presents as she's frightened for other folks to see.

Arthur (*trying to remain careless*) You're not only devilishly impertinent, you're talking nonsense! Every man likes to flirt with a pretty girl, and every pretty girl likes to be flirted with. The wider the distance between them, the less harm there is, for then she's not likely to deceive herself.

Adam (*quietly*) You know it couldn't be made public as you've behaved to Hetty as y' have done, without bringing shame on her and her relations. And what if you meant nothing by your kissing and your lockets? I tell you as you've filled her mind so with the thought of you as it'll mayhap poison her life, and she'll never love another man as 'ud made her a good husband.

There is a pause

Arthur Well, Adam, perhaps I've gone a little too far in stealing a kiss now and then. You're such a grave, steady fellow, you don't understand the temptation to such trifling. But you know I'm going away immediately — so I shan't make any more mistakes of the kind. Let's say good-night and talk no more about the matter. The whole thing will soon be forgotten. (*He turns away*)

Adam No, by God! (*He throws down his basket of tools*) No! It'll not be soon forgot, as you've come between her and me, when she might ha' loved me — it'll not soon be forgot — as you've robbed me o' my happiness, while I thought you was my best friend. You've been kissing her and meaning nothing, have you? And I never kissed her i' my life, but I'd ha' worked hard for years for the right to kiss her. You think little o' doing what may damage other folks so as you get your bit o' trifling, as means nothing. I throw back your favours, for you're not the man I took you for. I'll never count you as my friend again. Fight me, where I stand — it's all th' amends you can make me.

Arthur Adam, I don't want to fight you.

Adam No, you think I'm a common man as you can injure without answering for it.

Arthur I never meant to injure you. I didn't know you loved her.

Adam But you've made her love you.

Arthur Go away or we shall both repent.

Adam I won't go without fighting you. You're a coward — and a scoundrel — and I despise you.

Arthur hits out and they begin to fight. Out of the two, Arthur is more skilled but Adam is stronger

Arthur is suddenly floored completely and lies still

There is a pause, while Adam looks at Arthur lying motionless

G. Eliot/Actor 6 What had Adam done by fighting? He hadn't rescued Hetty, hadn't changed the past. He sickened at the vanity of his own rage.

Adam (*suddenly, to himself*) Good God!

He goes over and kneels beside Arthur. He lifts Arthur's head and tries to wake him but fails

G. Eliot/Actor 1 The horror that rushed over Adam completely mastered

him. He could feel nothing but that death was in Arthur's face, and that
he was helpless before it.

There is a pause. Finally Arthur shows signs of life

Adam Sir? Where do you feel pain, sir?

There is silence

    Do you feel any hurt inside, sir?
Arthur No, no hurt, but rather . . .

There is a pause

Adam Thank God, sir. I thought——
Arthur You thought you'd done for me, eh? Come, help me on my legs. I
feel terribly shaky and dizzy. That blow of yours must have come against
me like a battering ram. Here, I'll go to The Hermitage. (*He points*)

SCENE 19

The Hermitage. There is an ottoman

Arthur I don't suppose you knew I'd made The Hermitage a retreat for
myself . . . My hunting-bottle's somewhere. I'm tremendously in want of
some brandy-vigour.

They go in

Adam fetches some brandy and a lamp

*They sit opposite each other in silence. Arthur drinks and takes up a more
relaxed attitude*

Adam You begin to feel yourself again, sir?
Arthur Yes. I don't feel good for much, but I'll go home when I've taken this
dose.

There is a slight pause

Adam I'd no right to speak as if you'd known you was doing me an injury;
you'd no grounds for knowing it. I've always kept what I felt for her as
secret as I could.

There is a slight pause

    And perhaps I judged you too harsh—I'm apt to be harsh. And you may
have acted out o' thoughtlessness. God knows, it's all the joy I could have
now, to think the best of you.
Arthur Say no more, Adam. I forgive your momentary injustice—it was
quite natural with the exaggerated notions you had in your mind. We shall
be none the worse friends in future, I hope, because we've fought. You
had the best of it, and that was as it should be, for I believe I've been most
in the wrong. Come, let's shake hands.

Adam But I can't, till you've cleared up your behaviour t' Hetty.

Arthur I don't know what you mean, Adam. I've told you already that you think too seriously of a little flirtation. But if there's any danger in it — I'm going back to the regiment on Saturday and there will be an end of it. As for the pain it's given you, I'm heartily sorry for it — I can say no more.

There is a pause

Adam It'll be better for me to speak plain, though it's hard work. You see, sir, this isn't a trifle to me, whatever it may be to you. What I feel for Hetty is a different sort o' love. She's more nor everything else to me, all but my conscience and my good name. And if it's true — if it's only been trifling — why then I'd wait and hope her heart 'ud turn to me after all. I'm loath to think you'd speak false to me, and I'll believe your word, however things may look . . .

Arthur You'd be wronging Hetty more than me not to believe it. You forget that in suspecting me, you're casting imputations upon her.

Adam Nay, sir. You're acting with your eyes open, whatever you may do. She's all but a child as any man with a conscience ought to take care on. And I know she's been fixing her heart on you. But you seem to make light o' what she may feel — you don't think o' that.

Arthur Good God, Adam, let me alone! I feel it enough without your worrying me.

Adam Well then, if you feel it, I've this demand to make of you. I ask you t'undeceive her before you go away. I ask you to write a letter — you may trust to my seeing as she gets it — tell her the truth, tell her it's only been trifling and take blame to yourself. I speak plain, sir, but there's nobody can take care o' Hetty in this thing but me.

Arthur I shall take what measures I think proper.

Adam No that won't do. I must be safe as you've put an end to it. I don't forget what's owing to you as a gentleman, but in this thing we're man and man, and I can't give up.

There is a pause

Arthur I'll see you tomorrow. I can bear no more now. I'm ill.

Adam (*blocking his exit*) You won't see her again. Either tell me you've been lying and she can never be my wife, or else write me that letter.

There is a pause

Arthur Very well, give me pen and paper.

Adam gives him a pen and paper

Adam I'll leave you for a moment . . .

Adam goes

Arthur What else could I do but deceive him? (*He writes with reluctance*) Dammit, this letter's a barbarity. (*He stops*) I'll carry Hetty away and all other considerations can go to the devil. No, I've always seen it must end.

It's the greatest kindness I can do her, poor dear thing. (*He writes*) At least it's been a secret, and Adam will help us keep it. Sadness for Hetty is likely to be the worst consequence. Perhaps in the future I might be able to do a great deal for her, and make up to her. Her heart may really turn to Adam after a while, in which case there's no real harm done. Unless she becomes violent, or unless she . . . (*He becomes filled with a sudden dread*) I don't deserve that things should turn out badly. I've been led on by circumstances . . . (*He writes*) Adam!

Adam returns

Arthur seals the letter

I've written everything you wish. I leave it to you to decide whether you'll be doing best to deliver it to Hetty. Perhaps . . .

But Adam is implacable

There'll be no need to see each other before I go.

Adam takes the letter and exits

Arthur groans and curls up on the ottoman. There is a pause

G. Eliot/Actor 5 Is this the same Arthur?
G. Eliot/Actor 6 The same, under different conditions.
G. Eliot/Actor 1 Our deeds determine us as much as we determine our deeds, and until we know what will be the peculiar combination of outward and inward facts which constitute a man's critical actions, it will be best not to think ourselves wise about his character.

There is a pause

Arthur God, what a miserable fool I am. And yet if ever a man had excuses, I have . . .
G. Eliot/Actor 5 Pity that consequences are determined, not by excuses, but by actions.

SCENE 20

The Hall Farm garden

Evening light

Adam faces Hetty

G. Eliot/Actor 2 It was hardly two months since Adam had had his mind filled with delicious hopes as he stood by Hetty's side in the garden at Hall Farm.
Hetty You've no right to say as I love him——
Adam I doubt it must be so, Hetty, for I canna believe you'd let any man kiss you by yourselves and give you a gold box with his hair and go a-walking i' the Grove to meet him, if you didna love him. I'm not

blaming you — it's him I blame for stealing your love i' that way. He's been making a plaything of you and caring nothing.

Hetty (*in pain and anger*) He does care for me.

Adam Nay Hetty——

Hetty I know better nor you——

Adam —he told me himself. I can't help thinking as you've been trusting t's loving you well enough to marry you for all he's a gentleman; but it's never entered his head, the thought o' marrying you.

Hetty How do you know? How durst you say so?

Adam I've got a letter i' my pocket as he wrote himself. He says he's told you the truth in it. (*He brings out the letter but holds it back from her*) Hetty, don't let it take too much hold on you. It wouldn't ha' been good for you if he'd wanted to marry you. It 'ud ha' led to no happiness i' the end. (*Slight pause*) Don't bear me ill-will, Hetty, because I'm bringing you this pain. There's nobody but me knows about this, and I'll take care of you as if I was your brother. You're the same as ever to me, for I don't believe you've done any wrong knowingly.

She puts the letter in her pocket and exits

Her head was allays likely to be turned by a gentleman — with his fine clothes, and white hands, and that way o' talking — making up to her in a bold way as a man couldn't do that was only her equal — and it's much if she'll ever like a common man now. (*He looks at his hands*) I'm a roughish fellow altogether. I don't know what there is much for a woman to like about me. Yet there's no telling. I must put up with it, whichever way it is and be thankful it's been no worse. I'm not th' only man that's got to do without much happiness i' this life.

SCENE 21

A divided stage — on one side of the stage a light on Adam reading a letter at the Bedes' cottage

Lisbeth What ails Adam, dost know Seth? He's like as if he was struck for death this day or two, he's so cast down.

Seth He's a deal o' work upon him just now, Mother, and I think he's a bit troubled in his mind. Don't you take notice of it because it hurts him when you do. Don't say anything to vex him.

Lisbeth Eh; what dost talk o' my vexing him?

Seth He's reading the letter Dinah wrote me. I thought perhaps it 'ud comfort him.

Lisbeth I'll ma' him a kettle-cake for breakfast i' the morning.

Dimly now we can see Dinah

Dinah. . . in my outward lot, I have all things and abound. I have had constant work in the mill, and my body is greatly strengthened. What you say about staying in your own country ∧with your mother and brother ,Seth,

∧

shows me that you have a true guidance. I was thankful for your tidings about Hall Farm. Often the thought of them is borne in on me as if they were in need and trouble which yet is dark to me. There may be some leading here, but I wait to be taught. You say they are all well . . . Tell your mother I often bear her in my thoughts at evening time when I'm sitting in the dim light as I did with her. That's a blessed time, isn't it Seth, when the outward light is fading and the body is wearied with work. I sit on my chair in the dark room and close my eyes and then, the very hardship and the sorrow I have beheld — yea, all the anguish which sometimes wraps me round like a sudden darkness — I can bear with a willing pain. For I feel it, I feel it, Infinite Love is suffering too, yea in the fullness of knowledge it suffers. Sorrow is a part of love and love doesn't seek to throw it off. . .

Crossfade to the other half of the stage. A light on Hetty, alone in her bedroom

Hetty How's Adam to know what's in Arthur's letter? (*She kisses the letter, then opens it and reads*)

Dimly now we can see Arthur

Arthur Dearest Hetty — I've spoken truly when I've said I loved you, and I shall never forget our love. If I say anything to pain you in this letter, do not believe it's for want of love and tenderness towards you, for I can't bear to think of my little Hetty shedding tears when I'm not there to kiss them away. But dear, dear Hetty, it's my duty to ask you to love and care for me as little as you can. The fault has all been mine. If I were to do what you one day spoke of and make you my wife, I should only be adding to the wrong I have done, besides offending against the other relations of life. And since I cannot marry you, we must part — we must try not to feel like lovers anymore. If any trouble should come that we do not now foresee, trust in me to do everything that lies in my power. But do not write unless there is something I can really do for you. Forgive me, my sweet one——

Hetty You're cruel, cruel to write so, cruel not to marry me, cruel. (*She breaks down and cries*)

The Lights come up. Hetty stands facing the audience

G. Eliot/Actor 2 She had no tears in the morning. Every morning to come, as far as her imagination could stretch, she would have to get up and feel that the day would have no joy for her.

G. Eliot/Actor 1 There is no despair so absolute as that which comes with the first moments of our first great sorrow, when we have not yet known what it is to have suffered and to be healed, to have despaired and to have recovered hope.

Fade to Black-out

ACT II

Scene 22

The Hall Farm

Mr Poyser Why, what's put that into your head, my wench?

Hetty I should like it better than farm work, Uncle——

Mr Poyser Nay, nay, you fancy so because you donna know it, my wench.

Hetty I should get good wages . . . I should . . . (*She starts to cry*)

Mr Poyser Hegh, hegh! Crying's for them as ha' got no home—not for
 . them as want to get rid o' one. (*To Mrs Poyser*) What dost think? Wanting
 to go for a lady's maid! We can do better for her nor that.

Mrs Poyser Maggots in her head! It's wi' going among them servants at the
 Chase. She thinks it 'ud be a finer life than being wi' them as are akin to
 her—she thinks there's nothing to't but wearing finer clothes nor she was
 born to, I'll be bound. And marrying one o' them valets as is neither a
 common man nor a gentleman.

Mr Poyser Ay, ay. We must have a better husband for her nor that, and
 there's better at hand. Come, my wench, give over and get to bed. Lets
 hear no more on't.

Hetty exits

I canna make it out as she would want to go away, for I thought she'd got
 a mind t' Adam Bede. She's looked like it o' late.

Mrs Poyser Eh, there's no knowing what she's got a liking to, for things
 take no more hold on her than if she was a dried pea. I can't ha' had her
 about me these seven year, wi'out caring about her. But a fool I am
 thinking aught about her.

Mr Poyser Nay, nay, thee mustna' make much of a trifle. She gets things in
 her head as she can't rightly give account on. Them young gells are like
 th'unripe grain, they'll make a good meal by and by, but they're squashy
 as yit. She'll be all right when she's got a good husband.

G. Eliot/Actor 5 And Hetty thought "Why shouldn't I marry Adam? I don't
 care what I do so that it makes some change in my life."

G. Eliot/Actor 1 She was ready for one of those convulsive actions by which
 wretched men and women leap from a temporary sorrow into a lifelong
 misery.

G. Eliot/Actor 6 As the weeks went by Adam found Hetty always pleased
 to see him and he began to believe her feeling towards Arthur much
 slighter than he had imagined. Perhaps her heart was really turning
 towards him.

37

Adam and Hetty enter

G. Eliot/Actor 2 Adam knew that the sight and memory of Hetty moved him deeply, touching the spring of all love and tenderness, all faith and courage within him.

G. Eliot/Actor 1 How could he imagine narrowness, selfishness and hardness in her. He created the mind he believed in out of his own, which was large, unselfish and tender.

Adam Hetty, I'm going to tell your uncle some news that'll surprise him, and I think he'll be glad.

Hetty What's that?

Adam Mr Burge has offered me a partnership in his business, and I'm going to take it.

There is a pause. Hetty looks upset

I could afford to be married now, Hetty — I could make a wife comfortable. Dear Hetty, what are you crying for? You think I'm thinking of Mary Burge — but I shall never want to be married if you won't have me.

She looks up at him and smiles

Do you really love me, Hetty? Will you be my own wife, to love and take care of, as long as I live?

She puts her cheek against his

G. Eliot/Actor 2 Adam could hardly believe in the happiness of that moment.

G. Eliot/Actor 5 Hetty wanted to be caressed. She wanted to feel as if Arthur were with her again.

Adam I may tell your aunt and uncle, mayn't I, Hetty?

Hetty Yes.

Mr and Mrs Poyser enter

G. Eliot/Actor 3 The red firelight on the hearth at Hall Farm shone on joyful faces that evening.

Adam I hope you've no objections against me for her husband.

Mr Poyser Objections?

Adam I'm a poor man as yet, but she shall want nothing as I can work for.

Mr Poyser Nay, nay, what objections can we ha' to you, lad? Never mind your being poorish as yet, there's money in your head piece as there's money i' the sown fields, but it must ha' time. We can do a deal tow'rt the bit o' furniture you want. (*To Mrs Poyser*) Thee'st got feathers and linen to spare plenty, eh?

Mrs Poyser It 'ud be a poor tale if I hadna feathers and linen when I never sell a fowl but what's plucked, and the wheel's a-going every day o' the week.

Mr Poyser Come, my wench. Come and kiss us and let us wish you luck.

Mr Poyser and Hetty kiss

There. Go and kiss your aunt.

Hetty and Mrs Poyser kiss

I'm as wishful t' have you settled well as if you was my own daughter, and so's your Aunt, I'll be bound, for she's done by you this seven 'ear. Come now, Adam wants a kiss too, I'll warrant, and he's a right to one now. (*Pause*) Come, Adam, take one, else y'arena' half a man.

Hetty and Adam kiss shyly

G. Eliot/Actor 4 It was a pretty scene in the firelight.

G. Eliot/Actor 5 Even Hetty felt something like contentment in the midst of all this love.

G. Eliot/Actor 4 Adam stirred no passion in her, but he was the best her life offered now — he promised her some change.

Mr and Mrs Poyser leave

G. Eliot/Actor 2 The next few months were a busy time for Adam and he could see little of Hetty except on Sundays.

G. Eliot/Actor 4 Two new rooms had been run up to the Bedes' cottage, for his mother and Seth were to live with them.

G. Eliot/Actor 2 It was a happy time, taking Adam nearer and nearer to March, when they were to be married.

Adam There's nothing troubling you, is there Hetty?

Hetty (*smiling*) No — I'm content and wish for nothing different.

Adam exits, reassured

G. Eliot/Actor 1 But all the force of Hetty's nature had been concentrated on the one effort of concealment.

Hetty Something will happen — it must happen — to free me from this dread.

G. Eliot/Actor 1 But now necessity was pressing hard upon her.

Hetty How can I hide it longer. I'll drown myself.

There is a pause

I daren't. I must run away where they can't find me.

G. Eliot/Actor 4 The possibility of going to Arthur was a thought which brought some comfort with it.

Hetty He'll care for me and think for me.

G. Eliot/Actor 4 Arthur was at Windsor. If he didn't mind about her as he used to do, he had promised to be good to her.

Mrs Poyser enters

Mrs Poyser Hetty — what do you think o' going to see Dinah and persuading her to come back wi' you, to stay over the wedding?

Hetty (*looking up hopefully*) Yes, Aunt. I'd like the change of going to Snowfield for a week or so.

SCENE 23

The journey

A coach is set up as simply as possible, using perhaps a table and stool

Adam I wish I could go with you on the coach and take care of you, Hetty. You won't stay much beyond a week, will you? The time'll seem long.
Hetty (*upset*) No.
Adam Goodbye. God bless you for loving me.

Adam exits

They set off

Coachman He's a pretty nigh six foot I'll be bound, isna he now?
Hetty (*frightened*) Who?
Coachman Why, the sweetheart as you've left behind, or else him as you're goin' arter, which is it?

Hetty is silent

Hegh, hegh! You munna take it too serious! If he's behaved ill, get another. Such a pretty lass as you can get a sweetheart any day. (*He laughs*) Steady there . . .

The same furniture becomes a table in an inn

Hetty Landlord! What places must I go through, landlord, to get to Windsor?
Landlord Well, Windsor; that's where the King lives . . . (*He shrugs*) You'd best go t' Ashby next — that's southard. But there's as many places as there's houses here in Stoniton. How comes a lone woman like you to be thinking o' taking such a journey as that?
Hetty I'm going to my brother, he's a soldier at Windsor. I can't afford the coach again. Do you think there's a cart goes towards Ashby in the morning?
Landlord There may be carts if anybody knowed where they started from. You'd best set off and walk and trust to summat overtaking you . . .

The furniture now becomes a cart

Hetty Mister? Could you take me up in your waggon if you're going south'ard? I'll pay you for it.
Cart-driver Well. If you dooan't mind lyin' a-top o' the woolpacks——
Hetty Thank you, mister (*She climbs up*)
Cart-driver I'm going no furder nor Leicester — and fur enough too.
Hetty Thank you.

The furniture now becomes an office

Clerk Windsor? Well, I'll tell you what I'll do. I'll write down the names of the chief places you must pass through. Er . . . Hinkley, then er . . . - Stratford, er . . .

Lady Bless me, you've come to Stratford-on-Avon. You wanted Stony Stratford — you've come a long way out o' the right road . . .

G. Eliot/Actor 1 It was not until the fifth day that she got to Stony Stratford. Here she determined to take the coach for the rest of the way, though it should cost her all her remaining money.

The furniture becomes a coach again

Windsor Coachman Here we are — Windsor! *The Green Man* at Windsor! Remember me, lady.

Hetty Can you give me back sixpence?

Windsor coachman No, never mind. (*He gives her back her last shilling*).

He exits. Hetty stands swaying

Windsor Landlord Come, young woman, come in and have a drop o' something. Here, missis, take this young woman into the parlour — she's a little overcome.

Windsor Landlady (*taking in Hetty's pregnancy and no ring*) Why you're not very fit for travelling. Have you come far?

They sit her down on a sofa

Hetty Yes, but I'm better now. Could you tell me which way to go to this place? (*She takes out Arthur's letter*)

Windsor Landlord (*reading*) What do you want at this house?

Hetty I want to see a gentleman as is there.

There is a slight pause

Windsor Landlord But there's no gentleman there. It's shut up. Been shut up this fortnight. What gentleman is it you want?

Hetty It's Captain Donnithorne.

Windsor Landlord Captain Donnithorne? Stop a bit. Was he in the Loamshire Militia? A young officer with reddish whiskers and a servant by the name o' Pym?

Hetty Oh yes, you know him — where is he?

Windsor Landlord The Loamshire Militia's gone to Ireland. It's been gone this fortnight.

Hetty faints. They lay her out on the sofa

Here's a bad business I suspect.

Windsor Landlady Ay — it's plain enough what sort of business. And she looks like a respectable country girl.

Windsor Landlord I never saw a prettier young woman in my life.

Windsor Landlady It 'ud have been a good deal better for her if she'd been uglier and had more conduct.

The Windsor Landlord and Landlady exit

After a moment Hetty opens her eyes

Hetty (*recovering slowly*) What can I do? I can't go into service now. I'll have to beg. Or go to the parish. (*In horror, she suddenly remembers her*

possessions and lays them before her on the sofa; the locket Arthur gave her;
→ *her ear-rings, ~~one shilling~~ and a red leather pocket book)* If only I could be
home again. Oh no, the shame. What can I do? I must get away from here
— get among the fields where nobody can see me. Then perhaps I shall get
courage to drown myself. (*She opens the red leather pocket book and reads*)
Dinah Morris, Snowfield. (*She considers*) She wouldn't turn away from
me.

G. Eliot/Actor 1 But Hetty shrank from going even to her. Afterwards other
people must know, and that she shrank from as from scorching metal. She
could only think of it as a possible alternative if she hadn't the courage
for death.

The Windsor Landlord and Landlady enter

Hetty (*offering them the locket and the ear-rings*) Can you give me some
money for these?

Windsor Landlord Well — I've no objection to advance you three guineas,
to get home with.

Hetty Oh — yes please. (*She takes the money*)

Windsor Landlady (*starting to try on the jewellery*) But if you want the things
again you'll write before two months are up, or we shall make up our
minds you don't want 'em.

*The Windsor Landlord and Landlady exit with the jewellery, and the sofa is
removed. Hetty sets off*

The Lights start to fade

G. Eliot/Actor 6 So she began to walk again, and take cheap rides in carts
and get cheap meals, going on and on without distinct purpose, often
sitting for hours under the hedgerows wondering if it were very painful to
be drowned, and if there would be anything worse after death than what
she dreaded in life.

G. Eliot/Actor 3 And then, there it was, a deep pool, black under the
darkening sky.

G. Eliot/Actor 1 There was no need to hurry, there was all night to drown
herself.

She stands on the brink, while the Lights fade almost to black-out

Hetty (*at length*) Curse you, Arthur. May you know desolation and cold
and a life of shame you daren't end by death (*She laughs, and then cries*)

Suddenly a Man is beside her in the darkness — a threat

Shepherd Yu'll be gettin' into mischief.

Hetty I'll keep in the road if you'll be so good as to show me how to get to
it.

The Man looks at her silently and then points

Hetty Thank you; will you please to take something for your trouble. (*She
holds out sixpence*)

Shepherd (*looking at it slowly*) I want none o' your money. You'd better take care on't else you'll get it stole from yer, if you go trapesin' about the fields like a mad woman a-that'n.

He goes and Hetty goes on

G. Eliot/Actor 3 She must wander on and on and wait for a lower depth of despair to give her courage.

G. Eliot/Actor 6 Perhaps death would come to her, for she was getting less and less able to bear the day's weariness.

G. Eliot/Actor 1 Yet, such is the strange action of our souls, drawing us by a lurking desire towards the very ends we dread; she took the straightest road northward towards Stonyshire and Dinah, and kept to it all that day.

SCENE 24

The Hall Farm and Adam's journey

Bright sunlight

Mr Poyser Ay, she's been too long.

Mrs Poyser Considering the things she's to get ready for the wedding — by the middle o' March!

Adam I'll go to fetch her. It's Sunday tomorrow. If I set out early and perhaps get a lift in a cart I could arrive the same day at Snowfield and bring back Hetty Monday; Dinah too if she's coming.

Mrs Poyser Small hope o' that unless you make her believe the folks at Hayslope are twice as miserable as the folks at Snowfield. (*Cheerfully*) Though you might tell her her aunt's wasted pretty nigh to a shadder.

Mr Poyser Nay, nay, thee't looking rarely. But I'd be glad for Dinah t'come, for she'd help wi' Totty . . .

Mr Poyser and Mrs Poyser exit

Seth enters

Adam Goodbye, Seth lad. I wish thee wast walking the way wi' me, and as happy as I am.

Seth I'm content, Addy, I'm content. I'll be an old bachelor, belike, and make a fuss wi' thy children.

Seth exits

G. Eliot/Actor 2 Seldom in Adam's life had he been so free from any cloud of anxiety. Every now and then he felt a rush of intense feeling towards Hetty and a wonderful thankfulness that all this happiness was given to him.

G. Eliot/Actor 5 That this life has such sweetness in it.

G. Eliot/Actor 1 At last he came in sight of Snowfield. Outside the grim steep town, Dinah lodged with an elderly woman.

Old Woman Will ye please to come in.

Adam moves forward and looks off eagerly

So you're come to see Dinah Morris? An' you didna know she was away from home then?

Adam No, but I thought it likely she might be away as it's Sunday. But the other young woman — is she at home, or gone along with Dinah?

Old Woman Gone along wi' her? Eh, Dinah's gone to Leeds — a big town you may ha' heard on — where there's a many o' the Lord's people. She's been gone sin' Friday was a fortnight. It's a pity ye didna know. Have ye come . . .

Adam But Hetty, Hetty Sorrel, where is she?

Old Woman I know nobody by that name.

There is a pause

Adam Did there come no young woman here — very young and pretty, Friday was a fortnight, to see Dinah Morris?

Old Woman Nay, I'n seen no young woman. Eh dear, eh dear, is there summat the matter?

There is silence

G. Eliot/Actor 3 Adam returned to Stoniton desperate to learn where Hetty had gone.

Adam stands centre stage

Other people enter and gather round

Girl No, no young woman like that's been seen here.

A Woman No, there's been no accidents to the coach on this road.

Coachman Yes, I remember her well. I joked with her that she'd left behind a sweetheart, or else she was going arter one. But I thought here was something more than common because she hadn't laughed when I joked her.

Landlord No, she never went by coach.

Coachman Never mind, I said — if he's behaved badly, get another.

Landlord She may have walked ——

Coachman I said, pretty as you are, you can get a sweetheart any day.

Landlord — I don't know which direction ——

Coachman But she never laughed ——

The Girl laughs

Landlord South ——

Lady Or north ——

Girl (*laughing*) Or east or west ——

Coachman But she never laughed ——

Landlord Face up to't.

All She's not to be traced further.

There is a slight pause

Adam (*to himself*) She's run away to Arthur. She's gone to him.

At the Bedes' cottage

G. Eliot/Actor 2 It was Wednesday morning when Adam reached home.

Seth God have mercy on us, Addy, what is it?

Adam puts his arms round Seth and gives in to his grief

Seth Is it death, Adam? Is she dead?

Adam No lad, but she's gone — gone away from us. She's never been to Snowfield. I can't find out where she went after she got to Stoniton.

Seth Hast any notion what she's done it for?

Adam She can't ha' loved me. She didn't like our marriage when it came nigh — that must be it.

Seth I hear Mother stirring. Must we tell her?

Adam No, not yet. I must set out on another journey directly — after I've been to th' Hall Farm. I can't tell thee where I'm going, and thee must say to her I'm gone on business as nobody is to know anything about. (*He starts to go*) I must take all the money out o' the tin box, lad; but if anything happens to me, all the rest'll be thine to take care o' Mother with.

Seth Brother: I don't believe you'll do anything as you can't ask God's blessing on.

Adam Nay, lad, don't be afraid. I'm for doing nought but what's a man's duty.

SCENE 25

The Rectory

G. Eliot/Actor 2 After he'd told of Hetty's flight at Hall Farm an impulse came to Adam to go to Mr Irwine and make a confidant of him. He was about to start on a long journey by sea and no soul would know where he was gone.

Adam waits for Mr Irwine

Adam Suppose something happened to me? Or I needed help for Hetty? (*Slight pause*) It's the right thing. I can't stand alone in this way any longer.

Suddenly Mr Irwine enters in a great state of tension. He is holding a letter, which he has obviously just read

Mr Irwine Adam, sit down.

Adam Mr Irwine, sir, I've something very painful to tell you.

Mr Irwine Yes, I've something too that very much concerns you — but please ——

Adam You was t'ha' married me and Hetty Sorrel, you know sir, on the fifteenth o' this month. I was the happiest man i' the parish, but a dreadful blow's come upon me.

Mr Irwine Yes?

Adam She's gone away, sir, and we don't know where. She said she was going to Snowfield o' Friday was a fortnight, and she took the coach to Stoniton and beyond that I can't trace her. But now I'm going on a long journey to look for her, and I can't trust t' anybody but you where I'm going.

Mr Irwine Have you no idea of the reason why she went away?

Adam It's plain enough she didn't want to marry me when it came so near. But there's something else I must tell you, sir. There's somebody else concerned besides me.

Mr Irwine (*almost relieved*) Somebody else? . . . Ah . . .

Adam (*finding it difficult to speak*) You know who's the man I've reckoned my greatest friend and used to be proud to think as I should pass my life o' working for him, and had felt so ever since we were lads——

Mr Irwine (*shocked*) Don't say that, for God's sake! No, go on—I must know.

Adam .... that man played with Hetty's feelings and it's on my mind as he's been false to me and 'ticed her away and she's gone to him, and I'm going now to Ireland to find out—for I can never go to work again till I know what's become of her.

There is a pause

Mr Irwine Adam, my dear friend, you've had some hard trials in your life. And yet there's a heavier sorrow coming upon you than any you have yet known. But I see now you're not guilty—you've not the worst of all sorrows. God help him who has.

There is a slight pause

Adam Sir?

Mr Irwine I've had news of Hetty just now. She's not gone to him. She's at Stoniton.

Adam rises

Wait, Adam, wait. She's in a very unhappy position—one which will make it worse for you to find her, my poor friend, than to have lost her forever.

There is a pause

Adam Tell me.

Mr Irwine She's been arrested. She's in prison.

Adam (*insulted*) For what?

Mr Irwine For a great crime. The murder of her child.

There is silence

Adam It can't be. She never had a child. She can't be guilty. Who says it?

Mr Irwine Here's a letter from the magistrate before whom she was taken. She'll not confess her name, or where she comes from, but I fear there can be no doubt it is Hetty. She had a red pocket book——

Adam But what proof have they got against her?

Mr Irwine Terrible proof that she was under the temptation to commit the crime—but we have room to hope that she didn't really commit it. Try to read the letter, Adam.

Adam takes it and tries to read it

We can still hope she's innocent.

Adam (*throwing the letter down*) It's *his* doing! If there's been any crime it's at his door, not at hers. Let 'em put him on trial—and I'll tell 'em how he got hold of her heart and 'ticed her t' evil and then lied to me. Is he to go free while they lay all the punishment on her?—So weak and so young. (*Pause*) I can't bear it. Oh God, it's too hard to lay upon me—it's too hard to think she's wicked. (*To himself*) She can't ha' done it. It was fear made her hide it . . . I forgive thee Hetty . . . Thee was deceived too. I'll go to him—I'll drag him back—I'll make him go and look at her in her misery . . . As long as he lives——

Mr Irwine No, Adam, no. Stay and see what good can be done for her. Don't go on a useless errand of vengeance. Besides, he's no longer in Ireland, he must be on his way home already for his grandfather's very ill and wrote for him to come, some days ago. I want you to go with me to Stoniton. Let's ride as soon as you can compose yourself. (*Pause*) There are others to think of and act for besides yourself, Adam. There are the Poysers on whom this stroke will fall more heavily than I can bear to think. I expect it from your strength of mind, Adam. (*Pause*) You will go with me?

Adam Yes, sir, I'll do what you think right.

SCENE 26

At Hayslope

G. Eliot/Actor 3 Soon, the Hall Farm was a house of mourning; the scorching sense of disgrace neutralised all other sensibility . . .

Mr Poyser I'll not go nigh her nor ever see her again. She's made our bread bitter to us for all our lives to come.

Mrs Poyser There's no staying in this country for us now.

Mr Poyser An' me as thought I should be glad when the young squire came to be our landlord. I'll ne'er lift my hat to 'im again, nor sit i' the same church wi' 'im.

G. Eliot/Actor 4 And at the cottage . . .

Lisbeth Eh, there's no comfort for us i' this world anymore.

Seth Shall I fetch Dinah from Leeds, Mother?

Lisbeth Ay, write a letter canstna'; she'd happen to know some good i' all this trouble. Eh, my lad—Adam my poor lad.

G. Eliot/Actor 6 And all through Hayslope and Broxton, the bitter waters spread . . .

Woman Do you think the creatur's guilty o' murder then?

Bartle Massey The sooner such women are put out o' the world the better.

Second Woman Ay, and the men that help 'em to do mischief had better go along with 'em for that matter.

Man (*shocked*) That's the young squire!

Third Woman Captain Donnithorne!

Second Woman He's the one that should suffer.

Man Ay, he's the one!

Woman Do you think they'll hang her?

Man It'll go hard with her. They say she denies everything, even denies she's had a child in the face of the most positive evidence.

Bartle Massey I don't value her a rotten nut, not a rotten nut.

Woman Adam Bede still believes she's innocent of murder.

They fall silent as:

Adam enters and passes between them. When he has gone:

2nd Woman The poor lad ——

Bartle Massey Ay, the poor lad . . .

SCENE 27

Adam's room in Stoniton

There is just a bed and window — like a cell

Adam waits

G. Eliot/Actor 2 An upper room in a dull Stoniton street, where Adam decided to take lodgings until the trial was over.

Mr Irwine enters

Adam goes quickly to meet him

Adam Have you seen her, sir?

Mr Irwine Yes, Adam, and I said you wished to see her before the trial tomorrow, if she consented.

Adam And?

Mr Irwine You know she shrinks from seeing anyone, Adam. It's not only you — some fatal influence seems to have shut up her heart. She only shuddered and said "No!" in the same cold, obstinate way as usual. I fear a meeting would be pure useless suffering to you. She is very much changed.

Adam rises suddenly and goes for the door — Mr Irwine blocks the way

Adam Is he come back?

Mr Irwine No, he's not.

Adam You needn't deceive me, sir. I only want justice ——

Mr Irwine I'm not deceiving you, Adam. When I left Hayslope, Arthur Donnithorne was not come back. I've left a letter for him. He'll know all, as soon as he arrives.

Adam But you don't mind about it. You think it doesn't matter as she lies there in shame and he suffers nothing.

Mr Irwine Adam, he will suffer. This will be a shock of which he'll feel the effects all his life. Why do you crave vengeance in this way? No amount of torture that you could inflict on him could benefit her.

Adam Oh God, no! That's what makes the blackness of it. It can never be undone. My poor Hetty. (*Abruptly*) But she isn't as guilty as they say? She can't ha' done it.

Mr Irwine But suppose the worst. You have no right to say the guilt of her crime lies with him. The evil consequences that may lie folded in a single act of selfish indulgence is a thought so awful that it ought surely to awaken some feeling less presumptous than a rash desire to punish. If you were to obey your passion for revenge — for it *is* passion and you deceive yourself in calling it justice — it might be with you precisely as it has been with Arthur — nay, worse ——

Adam No, not worse ——

Mr Irwine — your passion might lead you, yourself, to a horrible crime ——

Adam I don't believe it's worse. I'd sooner do a wickedness as I could suffer for by myself than ha' brought *her* to do wickedness — and all for a bit o' pleasure ——

Mr Irwine But there's no sort of wrong deed of which a man can bear the punishment alone. You can't isolate the evil in you. Men's lives are as thoroughly blended with each other as the air they breathe. An act of blind fury would leave all the present evils just as they are and add worse evils to them. (*Pause*) Remember what you've told me about your feelings after you'd given that blow to Arthur in the Grove.

There is silence

Adam Is Dinah Morris come to Hall Farm yet, sir?

Mr Irwine No. They're afraid the letter hasn't reached her.

Adam I wonder if Dinah 'ud ha' gone to see her. The Methodists are great folks for going into the prisons. I wonder if she could ha' done any good.

Mr Irwine (*considering*) It's possible.

Adam But it's o' no use if she doesn't come.

SCENE 28

Adam's room in Stoniton

Adam sits on the bed

G. Eliot/Actor 5 The morning of the trial had arrived.

Hetty is lit by an unreal light. There is the sound of a drumbeat

Judge Do you plead guilty, or not guilty?

There is a silence. Hetty cannot answer

Counsel She pleads not guilty.

The light fades and with it the drumbeat

G. Eliot/Actor 2 But Adam chose now to bear the long hours of suspense in his room rather than to encounter the more intolerable agony of witnessing her trial.

G. Eliot/Actor 5 Energetic natures, strong for all strenuous deeds, will often rush away from a hopeless sufferer, as if they were hard-hearted.

G. Eliot/Actor 2 They shrink from the pain by an ungovernable instinct.

G. Eliot/Actor 1 Yet deep unspeakable suffering may well be called a baptism, the initiation into a new state.

G. Eliot/Actor 6 Bartle Massey, the schoolmaster, had shut up his school and had gone to Stoniton to help look after Adam, and keep him company.

Bartle Massey (*approaching*) I've just come to look at you, my boy, for the folks are gone out of Court for a bit. Mr Irwine sent this. (*He carries bread rolls and wine*) Come now, drink a drop with me, my lad — drink with me.

Adam Tell me all about it, Mr Massey. Have they begun?

Bartle Massey Yes, my boy, but they're slow, they're slow. And there's the counsel they've got for her puts a spoke in the wheel whenever he can, and there's . . . I'd have given up figures for ever only to have had some good news to bring to you, my poor lad.

Adam Does it seem to be going against her?

Bartle Massey Why, the chief evidence yet has been the doctor's — all but poor Mr Poyser's. Everybody in court felt for him. The worst was when they told him to identify the prisoner at the bar. It was hard work, poor fellow — it was hard work. Mr Irwine put himself near him and went with him out o' court.

Adam God bless him ——

Bartle Massey Ay, he's good metal, our parson. He's not one of those that think they can comfort you with chattering, as if folks who look on know the trouble better than those who have to bear it. I've had to do with such folks in my time, in the south, when I was in trouble myself.

Adam But the other evidence — does it go hard against her? Tell me the truth.

Bartle Massey Yes, my lad, yes. The doctor's evidence is heavy on her, is heavy. She's gone on denying she's had a child from first to last: these poor silly women-things — they've not the sense to know it's no use denying what's proved. It'll make against her with the jury.

Adam Tell me how she looked.

Bartle Massey White as a sheet.

Adam Is there nobody to stand by her? (*Pause. He stands*) It's cowardly of me to keep away. I'll stand by her — for all she's been deceitful. I used to be hard sometimes. I'll never be hard again. I'll go, Mr Massey. I'll go with you.

Bartle Massey Take a bite then, and a sup, Adam, for the love of me. See, I must stop and eat a morsel. Now, you take some.

They share the bread and wine for a moment

G. Eliot/Actor 1 A great anguish may do the work of years and we may come out from that baptism of fire with a soul full of a new awe and a new pity.

SCENE 29

The Court

There is the sound of a drumbeat and a bright light on the witness stand

We can dimly see Hetty, and Adam watching her

From the darkness come the voices of the Counsel and the Judge

The drumbeat fades

Counsel Your name?

Sarah Stone Sarah Stone.

Counsel And where do you live?

Sarah Stone I keep a shop in Church Lane here in Stoniton. That Saturday
night . . .

Counsel February twenty-seventh

Sarah Stone Yes. (*She points*) She came and asked for a lodging at my
house. She looked ill and tired.

Counsel You are sure it was the prisoner?

Sarah Stone Oh yes. Her condition, and something respectable about her
clothes, made me as I couldn't find it in my heart to send her away. (*Slight
pause*) In the night a child was born.

Reaction in the Court

Counsel Did you send for a doctor?

Sarah Stone There seemed to be no need.

Counsel (*holding up baby clothes*) Do you recognize these baby's clothes?

Sarah Stone Yes — I made them myself. I'd kept them ever since my last
child was born. I dressed the child in them.

Counsel And the next day?

Sarah Stone She would get up. She said she felt quite strong enough. But
I wasn't quite easy about her, and towards evening next day I made up
my mind to speak to our minister about it. I left the prisoner sitting up
by the fire in the kitchen with the baby on her lap. When we got back, the
candle was burning just as I left it, but the prisoner and the baby were
gone.

Reaction in the Court

Judge Stand down.

Silence, apart from the sound of the drumbeat

G. Eliot/Actor 2 And Adam thought "How can she be guilty? Else why
should she have taken her baby with her? She might have left it
behind . . ."

The drumbeat fades

Counsel Your name?

John Olding John Olding. I'm a labourer at Hetton Farm. I first saw the prisoner in a red cloak sitting under a bit of a haystack. She got up when she saw me and seemed as if she'd be walking on the other way. I thought she looked a bit crazy, but it was no business of mine. I had to go to the other side of Hetton Coppice.

Counsel What happened then?

John Olding I hadn't got far before I heard a strange cry. It didn't come from any animal I knew. For a good while I kept looking up at the boughs; and then I thought it came from the ground. I looked about, but could find nothing, and at last the cry stopped. (*Slight pause*) But when I came back the same way pretty nigh on an hour after, I couldn't help laying down my stakes to have another look. Then I saw something odd and round and whitish lying on the ground under a nut-bush by the side of me. And I stooped down to pick it up, and I saw it was a little baby's hand. (*A thrill of horror*) There were a lot of timber-choppings under the bush and the hand came out from among them. But there was a hole left in one place and I could see down it and see the child's head. I took out the child. Its body was cold. I made back home to my wife. She said it was dead and I'd better take it to the parish and tell the constable. And I said "I'll lay my life it's the young woman's child as I met going to the coppice." And the next morning another constable came with me to the spot where I found the child. And when we got there, there was the prisoner a-sitting against the bush where I found the child. She cried out when she saw us, but she never offered to move.

Judge Stand down.

There is only the sound of the drumbeat

G. Eliot/Actor 2 And Adam thought "She's guilty."

Judge Gentlemen of the Jury, what is your verdict?

All Guilty.

Judge Hester Sorrel. You have been found guilty of child-murder. You are to be taken to a place of execution and then to be hanged by the neck till you be——

Hetty shrieks and falls

Adam tries to reach her, but is too late

The drumbeat fades

SCENE 30

Arthur's return — bright daylight

G. Eliot/Actor 6 When Arthur first learnt of the old Squire's death he felt——

Arthur Poor grandfather.

G. Eliot/Actor 1 It's impossible to say that his grief was deeper than that.

G. Eliot/Actor 3 But it is not in human nature — only in human pretence — for a young man like Arthur, with a fine constitution——

G. Eliot/Actor 2 Thinking well of himself, believing that others think well of him——

G. Eliot/Actor 6 And just coming into a splendid estate through the death of a very old man whom he wasn't fond of, to feel anything very different from . . .

G. Eliot/Actor 4 Exultant joy!

Arthur Now my real life is beginning! I'll show them what a fine country gentleman is!

A coach is arranged for him. Arthur has his back to the driver

G. Eliot/Actor 5 Arthur was at ease about Hetty. Mr Irwine had sent him word that Adam Bede was to marry pretty Hetty Sorrel.

Arthur (*to the audience*) The little puss can't have cared for me half as much as I cared for her. I'm a great fool about her still—almost afraid to see her—indeed I haven't cared much to look at any other woman since I parted from her. Strange how long this sort of business lasts . . . I'm not in love with Hetty now, oh no—I've earnestly hoped she should marry Adam and *now* it's actually in my power to do a great deal for them. Thank heaven it's turned out so well! I should have plenty of interests to fill my life now and not be in danger of playing the fool again.

G. Eliot/Actor 5 Pleasant the sense of being swept along in swift ease through English scenes, till here was dear old Hayslope at last . . .

Driver Whoa!

G. Eliot/Actor 5 He was happy and would make everyone else happy that came within his reach.

Arthur tips the driver

Driver Thank you, sir!

Servants remove the coach and bring on an easy chair and a letter

Arthur greets them all warmly

G. Eliot/Actor 3 To Arthur it was nothing that the servants looked grave and sad.

Servant From Mr Irwine, sir.

Arthur (*with pleasure*) Ah, good . . . (*He sits, opens the letter and then reads it*)

Mr Irwine's voice I send this letter to meet you on your arrival, Arthur, because I may be at Stoniton, whither I am called by the most painful duty it has ever been given to me to perform. Any other words I could write at this moment must be weak and unmeaning by the side of those in which I must tell you the simple fact. Hetty Sorrel is in prison, being tried for the crime of child-murder.

Arthur is absolutely still for a time, then quickly leaves

Arthur (*calling back*) Tell them I've gone to Stoniton.

SCENE 31

Hetty's prison cell

A bed and a window

Hetty sits without hope

Dinah's voice Hetty.

No reaction

    Hetty — it's Dinah.

Hetty reacts slightly

Dinah enters

Hetty rises and stares at her like an animal, in silence

Dinah Don't you remember Dinah? Did you think I wouldn't come to you in trouble? (*Pause*) I've come to be with you, Hetty. . . not to leave you. . . to be your sister to the last.

Then they are in each others arms

There is a pause

Hetty's arms slowly drop

Dinah Hetty, do you know who it is?
Hetty Yes.
Dinah Do you remember the time when we were at the Hall Farm and I told you to be sure and think of me as a friend in trouble?
Hetty Yes, but you can do nothing for me — they'll hang me o' Monday. (*Pause*) It's Friday now.
Dinah No, Hetty, I can't save you from that death.
Hetty You won't leave me, Dinah? You'll keep close to me?
Dinah I'll stay with you. But here's someone else besides me.
Hetty (*looking about, frightened*) Who?
Dinah Someone who's been with you through all your hours of sin and trouble, who's known every thought you've had and all the deeds you've tried to hide. And on Monday when I can't follow you He'll be with you then. It makes no difference whether we live or die, we're in the presence of God.
Hetty Dinah, won't nobody do anything for me? Will they hang me for certain? I wouldn't mind if they'd let me live.
Dinah I know death is dreadful. But if you had a friend to take care of you after death — someone whose love is greater than mine ——
Hetty But I can't know anything about it ——
Dinah Because you're shutting your soul against him by trying to hide the truth. I love you, Hetty, but if you'd not let me near you, you'd have shut me out from helping you. Don't shut God's love out. He can't bless you till you open your heart to Him. (*She kneels*)

Slowly Hetty kneels too

Hetty, we're before God. He's waiting for you to tell the truth.

There is silence

Hetty Dinah, help me . . . I can't feel anything like you . . . my heart is hard.

Dinah Jesus, thou hast known the depths of all sorrow. Thou hast entered that black darkness and hast uttered the cry of the forsaken. Lord, rescue this lost one. She's clothed round with thick darkness; she can only feel her heart is hard and she is helpless. She cries to me; Saviour — it's a blind cry to Thee. I believe in thy infinite love . . . Breathe on her soul, and it shall arise. Yes, Lord, I see Thee coming through the darkness, coming like the morning, with healing on thy wings. Let the eyes of the blind be open. Let her see that God encompasses her. Let her tremble at nothing but the sin that cuts her off from Him. Melt her hard heart. Make her cry with her whole soul — "Father I have sinned" ——

Hetty (*crying out*) Dinah — I will tell — I won't hide it anymore . . . (*Pause*) I did do it, Dinah. I buried it in the wood — the little baby — and it cried . . . I heard it cry. I was so very miserable, Dinah. I tried to drown myself and I couldn't. It was partly thinking o' you made me come toward Stoniton, I didn't think you'd be cross with me, but then I began to feel frightened because I was so near home. And then the little baby was born when I didn't expect it, and the thought came all of a sudden that I might get rid of it, and go home again. It got stronger and stronger. And I walked on and on and there came the moon. Oh Dinah, it frightened me when it first looked at me out o' the clouds — it never looked so before. And I saw the wood a little way off and I thought I could hide the child there and go home and tell 'em I'd been to try for a place and couldn't get one. I longed so for it, Dinah, I longed so to be safe at home. I seemed to hate the baby — it was like a heavy weight hanging round my neck, and yet it's crying went through me and I daren't look at it's little hands and face. But I went —— (*She stops. She sits on the bed and shudders*) I came to a place where there was lots of wood chips and turf and I sat down on the trunk of a tree. And all of a sudden I saw a hole under the nut-tree, like a little grave. And it darted into me like lightning — I'd lay the baby there and cover it with the grass and the wood-chips. And I'd done it in a minute — and oh, it cried so — I couldn't cover it quite up. I thought perhaps somebody 'ud come and take care of it and then it wouldn't die. And I made haste out of the wood but I could hear it crying all the while — and it was as if I was held fast — I couldn't go away. And I sat against the haystack. But after hours and hours the man came and looked at me so, I was frightened and went on. And then there was a barn and I went to sleep — but oh, the baby's crying kept waking me. And then I turned back, I couldn't help it — it was the baby's crying made me go. I saw nothing but that place in the wood where I'd buried the baby . . . I see it now. Oh, Dinah, shall I allays see it? (*She shudders again*) I knew the way to the place, and I could hear it crying at every step. I thought it was alive.

I don't know whether I was frightened, or glad. I don't know what I felt
till I knew the baby was gone. Then I was struck like a stone with fear.
I knew I couldn't run away and everybody as saw me 'ud know about the
baby. My heart went like a stone. It seemed like as if I should stay there
forever. But they came and took . . . me . . .

There is silence

(*She shudders again and then bursts out*) Dinah, do you think God will take
away that crying and the place in the wood, now I've told everything?
Dinah Let's pray. Pray to the God of all mercy.

                                    SCENE 32

Adam's room in Stoniton

Perhaps distant Sunday church bells can be heard

G. Eliot/Actor 2 The eve of the execution, at Adam's lodgings.
Bartle Massey A visitor — wants to see you.

Adam turns sharply

Adam Dinah. Bless you for coming to her. Mr Massey brought me word
yesterday as you were come.

They stand in silence for a moment

Bartle Massey Sit down, young woman, sit down.
Dinah Thank you, I won't. Hetty entreated me not to stay long away. What
I came for, Adam Bede, was to pray you to go and see her. It should be
today, rather than in the early morning when time will be short. (*She
waits*) Though her poor soul is very dark, she's no longer hard. When I
told her you were in Stoniton she said "I should like to say goodbye to
Adam and ask him to forgive me."
Adam I can't — I can't say goodbye while there's any hope. I can't bring my
mind to it. There'll perhaps come a pardon, Mr Irwine said.

There is a pause

Dinah waits for an answer

I will come, Dinah. Tomorrow morning. I may have more strength to bear
it if I know it *must* be. Tell her I forgive her. Tell her I will come at the
very last.
Dinah I must hasten back to her. Farewell Adam. Our heavenly Father
comfort you and strengthen you to bear all things.

They clasp hands

(*To Bartle Massey*) Farewell friend.

Dinah exits

Bartle Massey Well, if there must be women to make trouble in the world, it's but fair there should be women to be comforters, and she's one, she's one. (*Slight pause*) It's a pity she's a Methodist. But there's no getting a woman without some foolishness or other.

The Lights fade as Adam paces up and down

G. Eliot/Actor 6 It was a long and dreary night.

Adam It's the very day we should ha' been married.

Bartle Massey Ay, my lad, it's heavy, it's heavy. But you must remember, when you thought of marrying her you'd a notion she'd got another sort of nature inside her.

Adam I know. How could I think any other way? And if he'd never come near her and I'd married her and been loving to her, she might never ha' done anything bad. What would it ha' signified — my having a bit o' trouble with her. It ud' ha' been nothing to this.

Bartle Massey There's no knowing, my lad — there's no knowing. The smart's bad for you now — but there may be good come out of this that we don't see.

Adam (*flaring up*) Good come out of it! I hate that talk o' people as if there was a way o' making amends for everything. Her ruin can't be undone.

Bartle Massey Well, lad — it's likely enough I talk foolishness. I'm an old fellow and it's a good many years since I was in trouble myself. It's easy finding reasons why other folks should be patient.

Adam Mr Massey, I'm very hot and hasty. I owe you something different, but you mustn't take it ill of me.

Bartle Massey Not I, lad, not I.

G. Eliot/Actor 1 So the night wore on in agitation, till the chill dawn.

Adam I must go to the prison now, Mr Massey.

SCENE 33

The street

People crossing the stage — a rope is set up

G. Eliot/Actor 3 In the streets the eager people were astir already.

Woman What's happening?

Hangman There's to be no pardon——

Man No reprieve?

The crowd pass on the news

Hangman The cart is to set off at half-past seven——

Woman Come on then——

Man There's to be no pardon . . .

Others It won't be long — make haste——

The stage clears into stillness

Adam enters one one side, and Hetty on the other, supported by Dinah

Hetty is shocked by the reflection of her suffering in Adam

Dinah Speak to him, Hetty.

Hetty (*like a child*) Adam . . . I'm very sorry—I behaved very wrong to you—will you forgive me . . . before I die?

Adam Yes, I forgive thee, Hetty. I forgave thee long ago.

Hetty moves towards him

Hetty (*frightened; still holding Dinah's hand*) Will you kiss me again, Adam, for all I've been so wicked?

They kiss —a lifelong parting

And tell him—for there's nobody else to tell him—as I went after him and couldn't find him—and I hated him and cursed him once—but Dinah says I should forgive him . . . and I try . . . for else God won't forgive me.

Hangman It's time.

→ *A crowd gathers again quietly.* The drumbeat.

Adam goes

Hetty is taken towards the rope

Dinah Let's pray, Hetty. Let's pray to God

→ *Hetty and Dinah whisper prayers. As she gets to the rope, Hetty sees something. She shrieks and clings to Dinah.* The drumbeat stops

Everyone looks, some are pointing

Dinah What is it?

G. Eliot/Actor 4 A horseman is cleaving the crowd at full gallop.

G. Eliot/Actor 3 The rider's eyes are glazed by madness——

G. Eliot/Actor 6 He has a paper in his hand——

G. Eliot/Actor 3 Holding it up as if it were a signal——

G. Eliot/Actor 4 It is Arthur Donnithorne carrying in his hand a hard-won release from death.

G. Eliot/Actor 3 A reprieve!

All A reprieve!

Intense excitement

Black-out, then Lights up

G. Eliot/Actor 5 A reprieve—but not a full pardon. Hetty was to be transported overseas.

SCENE 34

The Grove—evening light

G. Eliot/Actor 6 Adam was resolved not to see Arthur again. He had learnt to dread the violence of his own feeling. But next day in the Grove . . .

Adam enters to look at the beech tree

Arthur enters

They see each other across the space

Arthur Adam. (*Pause*) I know it's painful to you to meet me, but it's not likely to happen again for years to come ——

Adam No sir. It would be better all dealings should be at an end between us and somebody else put in my place. I'm going to leave this part of the country ——

Arthur But something may be done to lessen the evil consequences of the past to others and you can help me. Will you listen patiently?

There is a slight pause

Adam Yes sir. Anger'll mend nothing, I know.

Arthur I was going to The Hermitage (*He indicates*) We can talk better there.

They go off

SCENE 35

The Hermitage

Arthur fetches the lamp

G. Eliot/Actor 6 The Hermitage had never been entered since they last left it.

Arthur I'm going away, Adam; I've chosen to serve abroad. (*Slight pause*) One of my reasons for going away is that no-one else may leave Hayslope on my account. There's no sacrifice I wouldn't make to prevent the consequences of ——

Adam The time's past for that, sir. A deadly wound can't be cured with favours.

Arthur Favours! How could you suppose I mean that? But the Poysers —Mr Irwine tells me they mean to leave Hall Farm where they've lived so many generations. Don't you see, as Mr Irwine does, that if they could be persuaded to overcome the feeling ——

Adam Folk's feelings are not so easily overcome. There's a sort o' damage, sir, that can't be made up for.

Arthur If I didn't care about what I've done, you'd have some excuse, Adam, for going away. But, when I tell you I'm going away—for years —when you know how that cuts off every plan of happiness I've ever formed . . . (*Slight pause*) If you would stay yourself and go on managing the old woods— you know that's a good work to do for the sake of other people besides the owner . . . (*Pause*) Mr Irwine's to have the chief authority on the estate—he's consented to undertake that.

Adam is silent

Perhaps you've never done anything you've had bitterly to regret of in your life, Adam; if you had you'd be more generous. (*He rises and turns away*) Haven't I loved her too? Didn't I see her yesterday? Shan't I carry the thought of her about with me as much as you will? And don't you think you'd suffer more if you'd been in fault?

Adam (*at length*) It's true what you say, sir. I'm hard—it's in my nature. But I've known what it is to repent and feel it's too late. I felt I'd been too harsh to my father when he was gone from me. I've no right to be hard. (*Pause*) I wouldn't shake hands with you once, sir, but if you're willing to do it now . . .

They shake hands

Arthur (*in a rush*) It would never have happened if I'd known you loved her. That would have helped to save me from it. And I never meant to injure her. I was all wrong from the very first, and horrible wrong has come of it. God knows I'd give my life if I could undo it.

They sit

Adam How did she seem when you left her, sir?

Arthur Don't ask me, Adam. I feel sometimes as if I should go mad with thinking that I couldn't get a full pardon—that I couldn't save her from being transported—that I can do nothing for her all those years; and she may die under it and never know comfort anymore.

Adam Ah, sir, you and me'll often be thinking o' the same thing when we're a long way off one another.

Arthur You *will* persuade the Poysers to stay, Adam, and stay yourself and help Mr Irwine?

Adam I'll stay, sir—I'll do the best I can. It's all I've got to think of now—to do my work well.

Arthur Then we'll part now, Adam.

They stand

Adam God bless you, sir.

They shake hands again

G. Eliot/Actor 6 It would be a poor result of all our anguish and our wrestling if we won nothing but our old selves at the end of it—if we could return to the same blind loves, the same self-confident blame, the same light thoughts of human suffering—

G. Eliot/Actor 5 —the same frivolous gossip over blighted human lives, the same feeble sense of that unknown towards which we have sent forth irrepressible cries in our loneliness.

G. Eliot/Actor 3 Let us rather be thankful that our sorrow lives in us as an indestructible force, only changing its form, as forces do, and passing from pain into sympathy—the one poor word which includes all our best insight and our best love.

G. Eliot/Actor 2 But there was still a great remnant of pain in Adam yet which he felt would subsist as long as *her* pain was not a memory, but an existing thing, which he must think of as renewed with the light of every new morning.

Scene 36

The Hall Farm Kitchen

G. Eliot/Actor 2 Now Adam was in the second autumn of his sorrow, and after eighteen months, Dinah, who had stayed to be a comfort at Hall Farm, was to return to Snowfield.

Adam You can't be happy then to make the Hall Farm your home, Dinah? It's a pity, seeing your aunt and uncle are so fond of you.

Dinah Their sorrows are healed and I feel I'm called back to my old work.

Adam You know best. I have no right to say anything about my being sorry, you know well enough what cause I have to put you above every other friend I've got. (*Slight pause*) I shall think of you thirty miles off as much as I do now, for you're bound up with what I can no more help remembering than I can help my heart beating.

There is a pause

Dinah is upset and starts to go

Adam Dinah, you're not displeased with me for what I've said, are you?

Dinah Oh no, Adam, how could you think so?

Adam You don't know the value I set on the very thought of you. You know I do mind parting with you?

Dinah Yes, dear friend, I know you have a brother's heart towards me. But I'm in heaviness through manifold temptations: you mustn't mark me. I feel called to leave my kindred, but it's a trial, the flesh is weak.

Adam I hurt you by talking about it . . . I'll say no more.

Dinah (*returning*) Have you heard any news from Captain Donnithorne?

Adam Yes. Mr Irwine read me part of a letter yesterday. They say there'll be a peace soon, but he says he doesn't mean to come home for some years. One thing cut me a good deal. "You can't think what an old fellow I feel" he says, "I make no schemes now." He says he's best when he's a good day's march or fighting before him.

Dinah He's of a rash warm-hearted nature, like Esau, for whom I've always felt great pity.

Adam Ah, I like to read about Moses best. He carried a hard business well through and died when other folks were going to reap the fruits. A man must have the courage to look at his life so. A good, solid bit o' work lasts; if it's only laying a floor down, somebody's the better for it being done well, besides the man as does it.

They are close to each other

G. Eliot/Actor 6 Adam conceived no picture of the future but one made up of hard working days such as he lived through with growing contentment and interest.

G. Eliot/Actor 5 Love, he thought, could never be anything to him but a living memory, a limb lopped off, but not gone from consciousness . . .

G. Eliot/Actor 3 He didn't know that the power of loving was all the while gaining new force within him.

SCENE 37

The Bedes' cottage

Adam sits reading an illustrated bible. Lisbeth is busy around him

Lisbeth That's her—that's Dinah.
Adam The angel at the sepulchre? It is a bit like her. But Dinah's prettier I think.
Lisbeth Well then, if thee think'st her so pretty, why arn't fond on her?
Adam Why, Mother, dost think I don't set store by Dinah?
Lisbeth Nay. If thee wast fond enough on her, thee wouldstna let her go away.
Adam But I've no right t'hinder her if she thinks well.
Lisbeth But she wouldna' think well, if thee wastna' so contrary.
Adam What dost mean?
Lisbeth Why thee't never look at nothin', nor think o' nothin', but thy figurin' an' thy work, as if thee wast a man cut out o' timber.
Adam What hast got i' thy mind, Mother?

Lisbeth sits

Lisbeth Thee might'st do so as I should ha' somebody wi' me, to comfort me a bit, an' be good to me. (*Pause*) Dinah's just cut out for thee. What's it sinnify about her bein' a Methody? It 'ud happen wear out wi' marryin'.

Adam is shocked

Adam Mother, thee't talking wild. Dinah's not for marrying.
Lisbeth Very like, when them as she'd be willin' t' marry wonna ax her.
Adam Mother—if Seth's asked her——
Lisbeth She doesna want t' marry Seth—But she's all of a tremble when thee't by her. Thee thinks thy mother knows nought, but she war alive afore thee wast born.

There is silence

An' thee—thee't fonder on her nor thee know'st.

Adam rises in a daze

G. Eliot/Actor 2 Adam was amazed; amazed at the way in which this new thought of Dinah's love had taken possession of him. He went to find out Seth as soon as possible.
Adam Dost think she's quite fixed against marrying, Seth?
Seth If thee meant it about myself, I've given up all thoughts as she can ever be my wife. She calls me her brother, and that's enough.
Adam But dost think she might ever get fond enough of anybody else to be willing to marry 'em?
Seth Well, it's crossed my mind sometimes o' late as she might; but Dinah 'ud let no fondness draw her out o' the path as she believed God had marked out for her.

Adam But suppose there was a man as 'ud let her do just the same and not interfere with her and . . .

There is a pause

They look at each other

Seth Why, would'st like her to marry thee, brother?

Adam Would'st be hurt if she was to be fonder o' me than o' thee?

Seth Nay, how cans't think it?! Have I felt thy trouble so little that I shouldna feel thy joy. (*Pause*) Thee mightst ask her . . .

SCENE 38

The Hall Farm. In the kitchen

G. Eliot/Actor 6 How is it that the poets have said so many fine things about our first love, so few about our later love? Are their first poems their best? Or are not those the best which come from their fuller thought, their larger experience, their deeper rooted affections?

G. Eliot/Actor 5 Tender and deep as his love for Hetty had been — so deep that the roots of it would never be torn away—

G. Eliot/Actor 3 Adam's love for Dinah was better and more precious to him — for it was the outgrowth of that fuller life which had come to him from his acquaintance with deep sorrow.

Adam But if a new feeling has come into your mind, isn't that a sign that it's right for you to stay and be my wife?

Dinah Adam — it's hard for me — you know it's hard — but a great fear is upon me. It seems as if you were stretching out your arms to me and beckoning me to live for my own delight, and Jesus, the Man of Sorrows, was standing looking towards me and pointing to the suffering and afflicted. I've seen that again and again when I've been sitting in stillness and darkness. Adam, you wouldn't desire that we should seek a good through any unfaithfulness to the light that's in us.

Adam I'll never be the man t'urge you against your conscience. But I don't believe your loving me could shut up your heart — it's adding to what you've been before, not taking away from it. For it seems to me that it's the same with love and happiness as with sorrow — the more we know of it, the better we can feel what other people's lives are or might be, and so we shall only be more tender to 'em and wishful to help 'em.

Dinah is silent

You shall go where you like among the people and teach 'em — for though I like Church best, I don't put my soul above yours. And you can help the sick just as much, and be among all your own friends, and surely you'd be as near to God as if you were lonely and away from me.

Dinah Adam, there's truth in what you say. But since my affections have been set above measure on you, I've felt as it were a division in my heart. I must wait for clearer guidance. (*Resolved*) I must go from you. (*Slight pause*) But you'll strengthen me — you'll not hinder me?

64

Adam Let's go out into the sunshine and walk together. I'll speak no word to disturb you.

Adam and Dinah go

Mr and Mrs Poyser enter, and look after them

Mr Poyser Heyday! There's Adam along wi' Dinah. Why, what dost think has just jumped into my head?

Mrs Poyser Summat as hadna far to jump, for it's under our nose. You mean as Adam's fond o' Dinah.

Mr Poyser Ay. Hast ever had any notion of it before?

Mrs Poyser To be sure I have. I'm not one o' those as can see the cat i' the dairy, an' wonder what she's come after.

Mr Poyser Thee never saidst a word to me about it.

Mrs Poyser Well, I aren't like a bird-clapper, forced to make a rattle when the wind blows. I can keep my own counsel.

Mr Poyser But Dinah'll ha' none o' him — dost think she will?

Mrs Poyser Nay, she'll never marry anybody if he isn't a Methodist and a cripple!

Mr Poyser It 'ud ha' been a pretty thing though, for 'em t' marry.

Mrs Poyser Ah, it would ha' been.

→ *There is a moment of regret.*

G. Eliot/Actor 1 So Dinah went to Snowfield and Adam waited.

G. Eliot/Actor 2 But as the weeks passed, Adam was hungering for the sight of her.

G. Eliot/Actor 6 And when that sort of hunger reaches a certain stage, a lover is likely to still it, though he may have to put his future in pawn.

G. Eliot/Actor 3 At length he set out for Snowfield.

G. Eliot/Actor 4 He waited for her as she came home up the hill in the evening.

SCENE 39

At Snowfield

Dinah walks past Adam, as she doesn't see him

Adam Dinah.

Dinah stops but does not look round

Dinah.

Dinah (*turning*) Adam. (*She goes to him quietly*)

They stand looking at one another for a while

My soul is so knit with yours that it's but a divided life I live without you. Now you're with me I've a fullness of strength to do our Heavenly Father's will, that I'd lost before.

Adam Then we'll never part any more, Dinah, till death parts us.

SCENE 40

As Adam and Dinah kiss:

The rest of the cast, except Hetty, gather at the Church

Adam and Dinah stand in front of Mr Irwine

G. Eliot/Actor 6 In November, Adam and Dinah were married.

G. Eliot/Actor 2 There was a tinge of sadness in Adam's deep joy.

G. Eliot/Actor 1 Dinah knew it and didn't feel aggrieved.

G. Eliot/Actor 3 Lisbeth was too busy with her pride to devise a single pretext for complaint.

G. Eliot/Actor 4 Seth was serenely happy. He was to be tyrannised over by Adam and Dinah's children.

G. Eliot/Actor 6 And Mr Irwine was glad at heart. For he had seen Adam at the worst moments of his sorrow, and what better harvest from that painful seed time could there be than this.

They all celebrate, with the dance from Act I: Mr Irwine watches

At the height of the dance, all freeze

Light on Hetty alone, standing apart

G. Eliot/Actor 5 But Hetty died abroad, just when her sentence was ending and she was coming home.

G. Eliot/Actor 6 As Adam had once said to Arthur "There's a sort of damage that can never be made up for."

Fade to black-out

FURNITURE AND PROPERTY LIST

The action is continuous, so that props and furniture need to be conveniently to hand at the places where the actors will need them for the next scene. In some cases it may be found best to keep the actors' props and furniture onstage throughout, just at the edge of a defined acting area.

Table
Chair
Two stools
Two benches
Adam's toolbag and mallet
Lisbeth's knitting
Lamp
Two wooden bowls with wooden forks and spoons
Six pewter tankards
Hetty's basket with red cloth filling it
Handmirror
Ear-rings
Locket on a ribbon
Bible
Two blankets to transform benches into beds
Rich cloth to go over chair and ottoman (optional)
Rose
Bartle Massey's stick and glasses
Bread rolls wrapped in cloth
Hipflask
Pencil and paper for **Arthur**'s letter
Arthur's letter
Dinah's letter
Red leather pocket book
Magistrate's letter
Drum
Wine-jug
Wine-cup
Letter from **Mr Irwine**
Rope for execution. A hook may need to be fixed from which this can be hung
Quill for **Clerk**
Floorcloth for **Stratford Lady**

One basic costume for each actor should be enough. However, if the parts are doubled, minor characters may sometimes need a distinguishing prop or piece of costume.

LIGHTING PLOT

Property fittings required: nil

Various interior and exterior scenes

ACT I

To open: general cover (daylight) and house lights

Cue 1	**Dinah**: ". . . . wise and the rich?" *Slowly fade house lights*	(Page 1)
Cue 2	**Dinah**: ". . . does that mean you and me?" *Crossfade to interior of Bede's Cottage. Evening light*	(Page 1)
Cue 3	Sound of **Adam** hammering *Crossfade to the Green. Warm evening light which very slowly fades throughout the scene*	(Page 3)
Cue 4	**G. Eliot/Actor 4**: "As Dinah does." *Crossfade to Bede's cottage, with lighting dimmer than previously. Continue slow fade*	(Page 4)
Cue 5	**Lisbeth** brings a lamp *Bright area around lamp*	(Page 5)
Cue 6	**Adam**: "Ay, Mother." *Fade to night. Only the lamplight remains*	(Page 6)
Cue 7	**G. Eliot/Actor 1**: ". . . open the door again." *Bring up cold morning light*	(Page 6)
Cue 8	**Adam**: ". . . too hard on him, too hard." *Crossfade to Hall Farm. Bright daylight*	(Page 7)
Cue 9	**Mr Irwine**: ". . . for a poor man's wife." *Crossfade to Bede's cottage. Cold morning light*	(Page 12)
Cue 10	**Adam**: ". . . fall short of them in loving." *Crossfade to the Grove. Warm evening light*	(Page 13)
Cue 11	**Arthur**: ". . . the first thing tomorrow." *Change to a divided stage. Area of moonlight in* **Dinah's** *room and area of lamplight or candlelight in* **Hetty's** *room*	(Page 15)
Cue 12	**G. Eliot/Actor 6**: ". . . couldn't unburden her heart to Dinah." *Bring up bright daylight*	(Page 17)
Cue 13	**G. Eliot/Actor 4**: "The human soul is a very complex thing." *Dim slightly to church interior*	(Page 19)
Cue 14	**G. Eliot/Actor 5**: ". . . the "growing pain" of passion." *Crossfade to Bede's Cottage. Evening light*	(Page 20)
Cue 15	**Lisbeth**: ". . . afore her teeth's all ~~gone~~ Come." *Crossfade to Garden. Warm evening light*	(Page 21)

67

→ *Cue* 16   **Mr Poyser**: ". . . sit ye down, sit ye down."   (Page 23)
             Crossfade to Hall Farm interior. Evening light

   Cue 17   **G. Eliot/Actor 5**: ". . . miserable lot to Hetty now."   (Page 23)
             Crossfade to nightschool interior. Lamplight

→ *Cue* 18   **Bartle Massey**: ". . . old lame Bartle beside you."   (Page 25)
             Bring up bright daylight

   Cue 19   **G. Eliot/Actor 2**: ". . . behave more kindly to him."   (Page 30)
             Slow crossfade to warm evening light

   Cue 20   **Arthur**: "Here, I'll go to the Hermitage."   (Page 32)
             Crossfade to dim interior

   Cue 21   **Adam** comes back with brandy and a lamp   (Page 32)
             Add lamplight

   Cue 22   **G. Eliot/Actor 5**: ". . . but by actions."   (Page 34)
             Crossfade to warm evening light

   Cue 23   **Adam**: ". . . without much happiness in this life."   (Page 35)
             Crossfade to very dim interior effect, with spotlight on **Adam**

   Cue 24   **Dinah**: ". . . love doesn't seek to throw it off."   (Page 36)
             Crossfade to very dim interior, with spotlight on **Hetty**

   Cue 25   **Hetty**: breaks down and cries   (Page 36)
             Crossfade, bringing up cold morning light

   Cue 26   **G. Eliot/Actor 1**: ". . . to have recovered hope."   (Page 36)
→   *Black-out*
             Fade to

ACT II

To open: Hall Farm interior. Firelight
   Cue 27   **Hetty**: ". . . Snowfield for a week or so."   (Page 39)
             Crossfade to bright daylight

   Cue 28   **Hetty** sets off   (Page 42)
             Begin to fade lighting

   Cue 29   **G. Eliot/Actor 1**: ". . . there was all night to drown herself." (Page 42)
             Lights fade almost to black. Dim light on **Hetty** *only*

   Cue 30   **G. Eliot/Actor 3**: "She must wander on and on . . ."   (Page 43)
             Imperceptibly the stage lightens

   Cue 31   **G. Eliot/Actor 1**: ". . . and kept to it all that day."   (Page 43)
             Increase Lights to bright daylight

   Cue 32   **Adam**: ". . . she's gone to him."   (Page 44)
             Crossfade to Bede's Cottage. Cold morning light

   Cue 33   **Adam**: ". . . a man's duty."   (Page 45)
             Bring up Lights to bright daylight

   Cue 34   **Massey**: "Ay, the poor lad . . ."   (Page 48)
             Fade Lights to gloomy cell effect

   Cue 35   **G. Eliot/Actor 5**: "The morning of the trial had arrived." (Page 49)
             Dim Lights and spotlight on **Hetty** *alone*

Cue 36	**Counsel**: "She pleads not guilty." *Fade spotlight and return to gloomy cell effect*	(Page 49)
Cue 37	**G. Eliot/Actor 1**: ". . . and a new pity." *Spotlight on the witness stand. Perhaps a little light on* **Hetty** *and* **Adam**. *Otherwise dark*	(Page 50)
Cue 38	Drumbeat fades *Quickly change to bright daylight*	(Page 52)
Cue 39	**Arthur**: "Tell them I've gone to Stoniton." *Crossfade to gloomy cell*	(Page 53)
Cue 40	**Dinah**: "Pray to God of all Mercy." *Raise Lights slightly for* **Adam's** *room*	(Page 56)
Cue 41	**Bartle Massey**: ". . . without some foolishness or other." *Fade Lights down to night effect*	(Page 57)
Cue 42	**G. Eliot/Actor 1**: ". . . till the chill dawn." *Raise lights slightly*	(Page 57)
Cue 43	**Adam**: "I must go to the prison, now, Mr Massey." *Crossfade to street. Cold morning light*	(Page 57)
Cue 44	**All**: "A reprieve!" *Black-out. Then bring up spotlight on* **Hetty** *alone*	(Page 58)
Cue 45	**G. Eliot/Actor 5**: "Hetty was to be transported overseas." *Crossfade to the Grove. Warm evening light*	(Page 58)
Cue 46	**Arthur**: "We can talk better there." *Crossfade to dim interior*	(Page 59)
Cue 47	**Arthur** fetches the lamp *Add lamplight*	(Page 59)
Cue 48	They shake hands again *Raise Lights slowly*	(Page 60)
Cue 49	**G. Eliot/Actor 2**: ". . . with the light of every new morning." *Raise Lights to Hall Farm. Evening light*	(Page 60)
Cue 50	**G. Eliot/Actor 3**: ". . . gaining new force within him." *Crossfade to Bede's cottage. Evening light*	(Page 61)
Cue 51	**Seth**: "Thee mightst ask her . . ." *Crossfade to Hall Farm. Bright daylight*	(Page 63)
Cue 52	**G. Eliot/Actor 3**: "At length he set out for Snowfield." *Crossfade to warm evening light*	(Page 64)
Cue 53	*As Adam and Dinah kiss* *Raise Lights to bright daylight*	(Page 65) ← Not italics
Cue 54	At the height of the dance . . . *Quickly change to spotlight on* **Hetty** *alone*	(Page 65)
Cue 55	**G. Eliot/Actor 6**: "There's a sort of damage that can can never be made up for." *Fade to Black-out*	(Page 65)

EFFECTS PLOT

The first production used no recorded sound effects; music for the dance was provided by the cast singing a version of "Over the Hills and Far Away", while they danced. A larger cast might wish to include a musical instrument or two. The following cues are optional.

Cue 1   **G. Eliot/Actor 1**: "He resolved not to open the door again."   (Page 6)
          Sound of heavy rain, which fades as the Lights come up

Cue 2   **Dinah**: "Pray to the God of all mercy."   (Page 56)
          Distant Sunday church bells can be heard